WEIGHT TRAINING
Everyone

4th Edition

Joseph F. Signorile
Rich Tuten
Clancy Moore
Virgil Knight

Hunter Textbooks Inc.

Special Acknowledgments: Cover photo: Copyright 1988 by Tyler Cox. All rights reserved. Models for cover: Jodie Bowman and William Evans.

Inquiries should be addressed to:

⊞ Hunter Textbooks Inc.

823 Reynolda Road
Winston-Salem, North Carolina 27104

PREFACE

In the last fifty years, a phenomenal increase has occurred in the popularity of weight training: first, as a rehabilitation technique for World War II servicemen (bringing about a gradual acceptance by the medical profession), then as a training technique for athletes, and finally as a valuable tool for building and preserving physical fitness and strength for the general public.

It is because of this tremendous interest that the authors of *Weight Training Everyone* have decided to make available to the general public the experience and latest knowledge which they have acquired in developing strength for male and female athletes and students at four major universities and a noted National League football team.

CONTENTS

CHAPTERS

APPENDICES

Weight Training: Today And Yesterday

WHY WEIGHT TRAINING?

The odds are that you are presently asking yourself why you chose an activity involving so much "hard work." Actually, there are a number of good reasons why weight training appeals to so many males and females and why it is rapidly becoming one of the most popular methods of maintaining fitness. Researchers agree that many people are dissatisfied with the shape of their bodies. Weight training not only allows individuals to target specific muscle groups, it also allows them to dictate the type of change the muscle will make. As you read this text, you will learn that different patterns of lifting can cause different changes in the muscle being exercised.

If you are the type of person who discourages easily and must see observable gains, then weight training should be your cup of tea. The serious weight trainer can often measure gains after only a few short weeks. Since it is customary to keep close records of the amount of weight lifted for each exercise, you will be able to see exactly how much progress you are making in developing strength, tone, or muscle size. The sport also allows nearly limitless variations in the workout as the weight trainer varies his or her exercises to make the specific changes desired. The large "menu" of lifts and lifting patterns available should guarantee that you will never become bored with your workout.

In addition, since weight training involves simple movements which target specific muscle groups, you can begin to experience success early in your training. This cannot be said of other sports such as tennis or golf, which require years of practice before an individual can participate at a competitive level. And, unlike sports such as softball or basketball, you don't need to form a team to enjoy the benefits of a good weight training workout.

Another appealing feature of the sport is the limited amount of equipment needed. Of course, some of the machines pictured in this book are very expensive; however, a simple set of weights and bar will allow you to engage in an excellent program at a very modest cost.

If, on the other hand, you are already a serious competitor in another sport, weight training can improve your performance. A large volume of literature provides substantial proof that proper weight training techniques can improve your ability to compete. In fact, it is now commonly accepted in most sports that, given equal skill levels, the stronger athlete will be more successful.

Women should recognize that weight training can increase bone density and muscle strength. In fact, studies have shown that resistance exercise performed on a regular basis can reduce the levels of bone loss often reported in women as they age. And while on the subject of aging, senior citizens should also recognize the benefits that they can derive from this sport. Recent studies have shown that persons as old as ninety years of age can significantly increase their strength and mobility with regular weight training. A weight training program is now considered by many experts to be of more benefit to our older population than aerobic exercise, since stronger muscles can help the elderly to maintain balance and prevent falls. Once you have decided to begin lifting, you are involved in a true "lifetime" sport—and it's never too late to start!

ORIGIN OF WEIGHT TRAINING

Prehistoric man, most likely, had no need to weight train. In the hostile environment where he existed, the development of a strong, fit body was not a decision, but a necessity. Primitive life required hunting and gathering with the most inefficient of tools. Physical exercise and strength were necessary just to survive.

As humans developed civilizations with domesticated animals and improved tools, the physical requirements placed upon them were greatly reduced but they maintained their fascination with the human form. Paintings and sculptures from the early Egyptians and, especially, the Greeks, depicted athletes and their performances. City-states such as Sparta and Athens produced art depicting the perfect human body, attesting to the importance they placed on fitness. In addition, the great heroic figures depicted in their poems and stories, such as Achilles and Hercules, possessed strength beyond that of normal men, and it was this quality that made them heroes.

The members of these early civilizations understood the connection between fitness and exercise. In fact, the word *gymnasium* is derived from the Greek *gymnasion,* a place for exercise.

Possibly the most famous of these early lifters was Milo of Crotona. This incredible athlete was one of the first to practice progressive weight training. He did so by lifting a calf several times a week. As the calf grew and added weight, Milo also adjusted by building his muscle strength until eventually he was the only human strong enough to handle the fully grown beast.

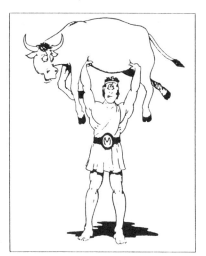

It is said that Milo's pride and strength ultimately caused his death. The story goes that the strong man was going through a deep forest and noticed a wedge deeply imbedded in a tree stump. Accepting the stump as a challenge, he attempted to tear it apart with his bare hands. However, as the wedge fell out, his hand or hands became caught in the vacated crack and he was unable to free himself. The tale has it that the animals of the forest eventually devoured him at the scene of his entrapment.

The earliest recorded weight training objects were dumbbell-like devices developed by the Greeks and called *halters*. The Irish had their own method which consisted of lifting huge boulders. Perhaps this is why Julius Caesar is reputed to have once said, "Forget Ireland; the Irish are wild men and will never make good slaves."

The term *dumbbell* is believed to have originated in England in the 1600s. The original versions were constructed by mounting regular bells, without clappers, on each end of an axe handle or stick—hence the term *dumb bell*.

About 1728, John Paugh, another early weight trainer, decided that apparatus involving dumbbells would be a valuable training aid. This concept was later adapted by Frederick Jahn, who founded the German gymnastics and strength movement.

This organization was later transplanted to America in the 1800s by migrating Germans and became known as the Turner Society, serving as a forerunner to the YMCA movement.

During the later 1800s, George Hackensmidt of Germany, who bent coins with his fingers, and other strong men like Eugene Sandow and Arthur Saxon performed in circuses and on stage. Unfortunately, many of these old time strength merchants did not present a desirable public image due to their being extremely fat. Because of this and the environment usually associated with weight lifting, the public indicated little interest in the sport during this era.

Undoubtedly the first Olympic games in 1896, and the succeeding games contributed greatly to the rising popularity of weight lifting and weight training. Until World War II, weight training continued to attract only a few professional strong men and a small group of competitive weight lifters.

The man most responsible for correcting these misconceptions was T.L. DeLorme, an American army doctor. DeLorme, while working with soldiers requiring physical rehabilitation, introduced weight training equipment and techniques. The results of his rehabilitation program caused the medical profession to change its opinions about weight training. This in turn led to acceptance by coaches and physical educators.

Thanks to the continued work of strength coaches, physical educators and exercise physiologists, strength training has become an integral part of all competitive sports. It is well known that resistance training can reduce the length of time necessary to recover from sports injuries and, in many instances, prevent their occurrence. One need only look at the number of gyms currently in operation in the United States and Europe to recognize that weight training is now an accepted form of physical exercise and has become an integral part of many lifestyles. The reason for this is simple—it works!

WEIGHT TRAINING TODAY

As late as the 1950s, weight training was confined to a select group of competitive lifters and bodybuilders. Weights were avoided by the general public as well as competitive athletes because of an unwarranted fear of becoming "muscle bound." With the advent of aerobic conditioning by Cooper in the 1960s, Americans became aware of the link between regular aerobic exercise, cardiovascular health, and weight control. A logical progression has led us to an understanding of the benefits offered by a regular weight training program.

Today's weight trainers can be classified into six basic categories:

Weight Lifters. Weight lifters are competitive performers with a primary interest in developing the techniques necessary for the two lifts used in Olympic competition—the two–hand snatch and the two–hand clean and jerk. They usually work at close to maximum resistance and rarely do more than three repetitions of any exercise at a given time. These athletes concentrate on extreme speed during each movement pattern. This is necessary since the competitive event requires the athlete to accelerate the weight as quickly as possible in order to complete the lift.

Power Lifters. These lifters have similar goals to those of the Olympic weight lifter. Their lifts are performed at high speed during competition, and training consists of few repetitions using extremely heavy weights. They generally compete in three power lifts—the squat, the bench press, and the dead lift; however, other lifts may be added during competitions called Odd Lifts Meets.

Athletes. A weight lifting program is now an integral part of every athletes training, regardless of the level of competition. There is considerable information proving that regular resistance training can improve athletic competition. It is important to remember that the lifts chosen should be similar in movement pattern and physiological demand to those required for the athlete's sport. This will be covered in detail in Chapter 12.

Body Builders. This group is most interested in developing massive musculature and great definition. The goal of their lifting is to sculpt the body by maximizing the size of each muscle, developing perfect balance across each body part, and reducing subcutaneous fat to maximize definition. This requires hours of lifting since a large number of exercises are necessary to target each muscle, and a large volume of work must be done to achieve maximum size and definition.

Patients. There are two basic reasons why doctors prescribe progressive resistance (weight training) exercise for a patient. The most important, from a medical standpoint, is the restoration of strength; however, a patient may be more concerned with his or her appearance rather than ability to function at 100 percent. Fortunately, the two often go hand in hand so that both objectives can be attained at the same time.

Jane and John Doe. This group is probably the largest of all, yet it often remains unnoticed since it is made up of the everyday males and females who lift for health, conditioning and recreation. It includes the high school student who wants to develop larger and more defined muscles, the elderly man or woman who wishes to strengthen muscles and increase bone density, college students who wish to remain fit while completing their studies, the middle-aged man or woman who finds that lifting adds to personal energy and self–image, and the recreational athlete who uses weights to improve performance. This group includes all of you who, for whatever reason, have chosen to begin a weight training program. The remainder of this book is dedicated to presenting the information necessary to help you accomplish this goal. All you need to do is read, and **hit the weights.**

Scientific Principles

MUSCLE PHYSIOLOGY

To develop an understanding of how weight training works, it is essential to recognize the physiological principles on which it is based.

MUSCLE STRUCTURE

The muscle itself is composed of a number of individual.protein building blocks which allow it to conduct electricity and contract. Of all the organs in the body, this is probably the clearest example of a pure structure–function relationship. This means that the structures of its proteins are perfectly suited for its job—to contract and make bones move.

Muscle is primarily composed of two amazing proteins, myosin and actin. When these two proteins come together, they cause both the release of energy for contraction and the mechanical movement itself. It is extremely interesting to examine the process of contraction, and it should help you to appreciate the changes you can make in this fascinating organ we call muscle.

MUSCLE FIBER

Each muscle is composed of many thousands of individual cells called muscle fibers. Each fiber is the thickness of fine thread and has its own separate nerve and contractile mechanism. Any changes in the strength and speed of a muscle are controlled by changes in each of these fibers.

All muscle fibers are wrapped in a connective tissue sheath which allows them to work as a single unit with the fibers around them. When they are examined under high magnification, they appear striped or "striated" due to the overlapping of their contractile proteins (see Figure 2-1). When viewed under the powerful electron microscope (see Figure 2-2), it can be seen that each fiber is covered with a series of "bumps," which are made up of two very different structures.

Figure 2-1: Light micrograph of skeletal muscle. (From *Skeletal Muscle Structure and Function*, by R.L. Lieber, Williams and Wilkins: Baltimore, MD. 1992. Used with permission.

Figure 2-2: Electron micrograph of a single muscle fiber (cell) showing nuclei and satellite cells. (From Bischoff, R., "Analysis of muscle regeneration using single myofibers in culture." *Medicine and Science in Sports and Exercise.* 21(5), 5164-5172, 1989. Used with permission.

One set of "bumps" are the nuclei of the muscle cell. These tiny structures are the designers of the muscle. When you exercise they receive information about the amount of weight you are lifting, how fast you are moving, how long you are performing the activity, and all the other factors involved. They use your needs to make the molds on which new proteins are produced. If you look at the number of nuclei on the muscle, and you realize that most other cells in the body have only one, you can appreciate how quickly and efficiently your muscles can change in response to the exercise you perform. This is biological "supply and demand," where you make the muscle work a certain way (demand) and it changes according to your wishes (supply).

The second set of "bumps" are a series of cells on the outside of the muscle called satellite cells. These can best be described as immature muscle cells that develop into fibers when there is damage to the muscle. The possible contributions of satellite cells during training will be described later in this chapter.

Inside the Fiber

As stated earlier, the two major proteins which make up muscle are actin and myosin (see Figure 2-3). Actin looks something like a twisted strand of rope, and myosin is shaped like your arm with a hand which can bind to actin, and a wrist and elbow which can

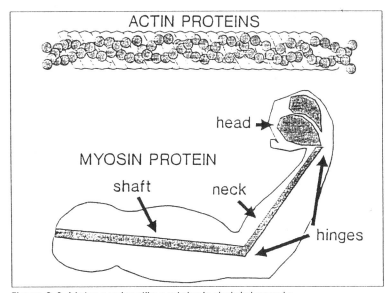

Figure 2-3: Major contractile proteins in skeletal muscle.

bend and pull the actin. To understand the way this works, imagine holding ropes on each side of your body and crossing your arms as you pull them in. The ropes would literally slide across you and anything attached to the ends of them would move closer together. If you tie a whole series of these ropes together, and have each in the hands of a separate person, all the people would move together and the overall distance between them would be greatly reduced. This is what happens to the proteins in your muscle when it contracts.

It should now become obvious that the more lines of people you have, and the more ropes you can pull, the more weight you can move. This is what happens as your muscle fiber grows during weight training. This growth is called **hypertrophy.**

Energy And Structure

The energy which allows the myosin "arms" to pull the actin "rope" is provided by a number of different systems depending on the activity. If you perform repeated activity at very low resistance, such as running or swimming, the muscle uses fats and carbohydrates and "burns" them in the presence of oxygen (aerobic). To accomplishment this, the muscle fiber must have:

1. a large number of blood vessels (capillaries) which supply the oxygen;
2. a large number of powerhouses (the mitochondria) which use this oxygen to burn the fuel;
3. thin fibers to allow the oxygen to easily pass (diffuse) into the muscle.

On the other hand, if you perform mostly heavy resistance short–term exercise, the muscle fiber produces systems which don't require oxygen (anaerobic). In this case, the muscle fiber has different needs which require different changes:

1. much thicker fibers to stand up to the higher weights;
2. structures which can break down carbohydrates very quickly to allow greater speed of movement (glycolytic enzymes).

Exercise scientists can examine muscle fibers and determine their properties by looking at their structure. This allows them to classify the muscles into various groups such as:

Slow Oxidative—having slow contractile speeds but the ability to contract for long periods of time with little fatigue due to their ability to use oxygen.

Fast Glycolytic—having fast contractile speed and very high force production but fatiguing very rapidly due to their poor oxygen delivery and utilization.

Fast Oxidative Glycolytic—having moderately fast contractile speed with moderately high oxygen delivery and utilization, and therefore, fair resistance to fatigue.

Although we don't know if human muscle can change from one muscle type to another during training, one thing is clear: muscle fibers can change their structure extensively in response to training. This ability to change makes weight training rewarding.

Muscle Plasticity And Training

Muscle is said to have a great deal of plasticity. Obviously this doesn't mean that it's made out of the same material as your typical model airplane or toy doll. What it does mean is that muscle has a tremendous ability to change structure and thus change function (recall the structure–function relationship).

If we force the muscle to do more work than it normally does (overload), over a period of time it will make the exact changes (specific adaptations) which the exercise demands. This is called training. For the muscle to continue to improve, it must be continuously overloaded as it adapts. In weight training, this usually involves increasing the weight as you improve. This is called "progressive resistance."

Specificity Of Training And Change

We can control five basic factors to force our muscles to change exactly as we wish—this is called specificity of training. Once you know what these factors are and how they affect your muscles, you can make the exact changes you desire.

The five variables are:

1. **Intensity.** How heavy is the weight you will lift?
2. **Frequency.** How many times a week will you workout?
3. **Duration.** How many exercises will you do? How many times will you do one complete movement (a repetition or "rep")? And, how many "sets" of reps will you do?
4. **Speed.** How fast will you move?
5. **Specificity.** What muscle will you target and what will you ask it to do?

Putting It All Together

Let's take a few examples using all the information presented above. You decide to lift a heavy weight, let's say 85 percent of your maximum. You do five repetitions, rest, do five more, rest and do a final set of five. What message is sent to your muscle, what change does it make, and how does it make that change?

Eighty–five percent of your maximum lift is fairly heavy; therefore, the nuclei of the muscle receive a message that says: "Make more actin and myosin—we've got a lot of weight to move." However, five repetitions take a fairly short time to complete. This sends a second message to the nuclei: "We don't need to use a lot of oxygen here—spend your time making the muscle larger, not better at delivering and using oxygen." Therefore, the changes made by the muscle would be to increase in size so it could produce more force, but not to expend a lot of its energy in making the structures that deliver and use oxygen.

If we look at the other extreme, where you decide to lift 50 percent of your maximum for three sets of twenty-five repetitions, as you can guess, two very different messages are sent. First: "This isn't too much weight, we still need to increase size, but not very much." And second: "This is taking a fairly long time so we need to make a better oxygen delivery and utilization system." In this case, the muscle would show a more limited increase in size, but much better endurance properties. Exercise scientists can actually measure this change in endurance by counting the number of mitochondria (those little "powerhouses"). He or she can also predict the speed of contraction of the muscle by measuring its levels of glycolytic enzymes (fast proteins).

These principles work no matter what changes you desire. The purpose of this text is to teach you which exercises affect certain muscles and how to vary your workout to get the exact changes you want.

How Do Your Muscles Grow?

We have now examined the changes that are possible and why they happen, but one final question remains: How do they happen? There are two ways in which a muscle can grow—the first, hypertrophy, has already been mentioned. *Hyper* means *exces-*

sive and *trophy* means *size*. When the muscle is used, it is required to make more proteins (myosin and actin) to become stronger. As stated earlier, these proteins are inside the muscle cell and are designed and built under the direct influence of the many nuclei which exist there. One interesting point should be made: we know that a number of circulating substances (hormones) can affect the growth of muscles, but we don't know how the muscles determine that they should begin to make more protein. Once this piece of the puzzle is put into place, we will have the link between overloading the muscle and seeing it grow.

The second possible way muscle grows is called hyperplasia. Literally, this means *more tissue*. This theory differs from hypertrophy because it doesn't say that new proteins are added to the old muscle fiber—it says that new muscle fibers can form. We know this happens with injured tissue in both animals and humans, and we have seen that it happens in animals during resistance training. Studies are now questioning whether it happens to us during training. Some of the latest data seem to indicate that people who do extensive training may be causing very small tears in the muscle and stimulating the little satellite cells, located on the outside of the muscle fibers, to become active and actually make new tissue. However, this theory still needs to be proven before it gains acceptance among exercise scientists, strength coaches, and physical educators. To date, the majority of the evidence does not support its acceptance.

No one can do everything. It's impossible to be a world class body builder and win the Boston Marathon. Like any worker trying to please the boss, the muscle has only a limited number of hours in the day to be exercised and to send messages for changes, then it needs to rest while these changes are made. Studies have shown that attempts to increase the endurance (oxygen-carrying) capacity of the muscle can reduce maximal strength and vice versa. What you need to do is set specific, realistic goals to satisfy your personal wishes while maintaining good health.

The Physics Of Lifting: Biomechanics

The first part of this chapter concentrated on the structural changes that could be made in a single muscle fiber due to training. This structure–function relationship can now be expanded to the whole muscle. An understanding of the mechanics of a lift will further explain why certain movements are so important to the activity.

From The Microscope To Your Muscle

One threadlike muscle fiber cannot move an arm or leg any more than one spoke can hold a bicycle wheel together. The whole muscle is composed of tens of thousands of muscle fibers. The fibers are wrapped into small bundles by connective tissues, and these bundles are wrapped together to make the whole muscle. At the ends of the whole muscle, all the connective tissue wraps come together to form a thick band called a tendon (Figure 2-4). Tendons connect muscles to bones.

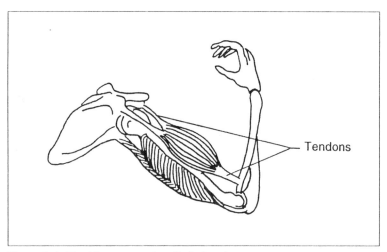

Figure 2-4: The biceps muscle with its tendons.

The whole muscle can take a number of shapes depending on its function and the bones to which it is attached. For example, the biceps muscle of the upper arm is a relatively straight muscle except for a splitting at the top which gives it its name, *bi-: two* and *-ceps: heads.* Since it parallels a long straight bone, it is shaped like a tube or cylinder with connections at each end. Its straight line structure tells you what it does—it moves the forearm directly toward the shoulder by bending the elbow.

However, the muscle of your chest, the pectoralis major, is a fairly flat muscle with a single tendon which attaches at the shoulder and many tendons which attach it all along your breast bone, the sternum. Since the chest must be an open space to make room for the heart and lungs, this muscle had to be spread out and flat to allow sufficient space for the number of fibers required to move the shoulders toward the midline of the body. So just as with the single muscle fiber, the whole muscle continues the structure–function relationship.

How The Whole Muscle Works

For your muscles to work they must be attached by the tendons to bones. You'd be a very mushy and flaccid individual if this were not the case. The bones themselves attach to each other at bendable areas called joints. This attachment of bone to bone is made by the ligaments. So when a muscle pulls on a bone, that bone pivots on another bone and a movement takes place.

The fact that muscle attaches to bone by a tendon means that when you weight train, not only the muscle, but the tendon and bone are also trained. Therefore, both bones and tendons will become thicker and stronger when you weight train. This is especially important as you grow older and begin to lose some of your bone mass. We now know that the thicker the bones are when you are young, the more bone you will have as you age. This is especially important to women because of the natural bone loss (osteoporosis) which occurs in later life.

Biomechanics: The Talk Of The Gym

Weight trainers use a number of biomechanical terms to describe the different movements performed by the body during a workout. For example, when a muscle contracts it can either shorten (raising a weight) or lengthen (lowering a weight). If the muscle shortens it is called a **concentric** contraction, if it lengthens it is called an **eccentric** contraction or "negative." Interestingly, the term negative is based on an imaginary physical line, called a vector, which is used to describe both the **amount of weight** moved and the **direction** in which it is moved. Since we are "weight lifting" when we train, the raising of the weight (concentric) is considered a "positive" movement and the lowering of a weight (eccentric) is considered a "negative" (see Figure 2-5).

This entire discussion would be academic except for the fact that most knowledgeable weight trainers tend to emphasize the negative portion of the lift and many perform "negative only" lifts. As with the other techniques which have been discussed, there is good scientific evidence behind this practice. First, it is obvious that more weight can be lowered than can be lifted, so negative only lifts, where a partner helps with the concentric movements and the lifter only lowers the weight, allow greater overload and,

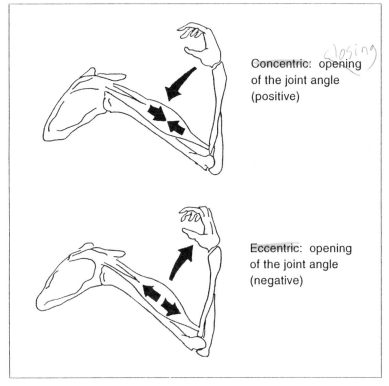

Concentric: opening [closing] of the joint angle (positive)

Eccentric: opening of the joint angle (negative)

Figure 2-5: Concentric and eccentric contractions.

therefore, greater improvement. And secondly, it has been shown in a number of studies that this negative or "eccentric" movement puts greater physical stress on the muscle, and is therefore superior in increasing its strength and size. "Negative" training techniques will be discussed further in Chapter 3.

The terms *agonist* and *antagonist* are also mentioned very often among weight trainers. The **agonist** is the muscle which performs the lift, while the **antagonist** is the muscle on the other side of the bone which opposes the movement and thereby keeps the joint intact (see Figure 2-6). Again, these terms carry practical importance for the weight trainer. Since antagonist muscles oppose each other across joints, it is important to work both muscles equally to maintain balance (symmetry) and reduce the possibility of injury.

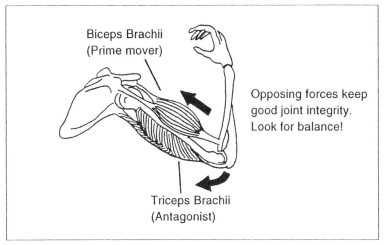

Biceps Brachii
(Prime mover)

Opposing forces keep good joint integrity. Look for balance!

Triceps Brachii
(Antagonist)

Figure 2-6: Prime mover and antagonist.

Flexion and *extension* are terms used to describe the action at a joint. Figure 2-7 illustrates each of these movements. An exercise where the angle of the joint is closed is called **flexion.** The most common exercises which employ flexion are movements such as arm curls and leg curls. **Extension** exercises use the muscle on the other side of the joint to open the angle. These are either extension or pressing exercises, such as leg extension and leg press exercises illustrated in a later chapter of this book.

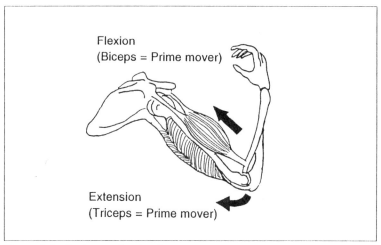

Figure 2-7: Flexion and extension.

The terms **adduction** *(ad=toward, duction=movement)* and **abduction** *(ab=away, duction=movement)* are also used to describe movement toward and away from the center line of the body (Figure 2-8).

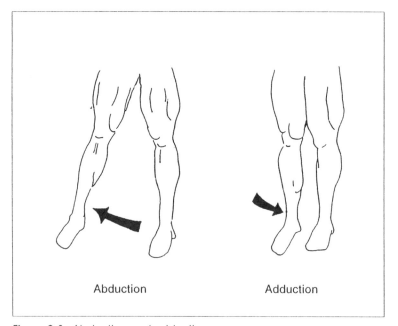

Figure 2-8: Abduction and adduction.

Leverage And Contraction

As these movements are discussed, another biomechanical concept should be mentioned. If we want to move a large rock, we can place a small rock next to it and then place a pole over the small rock and under the large one, creating a lever to move the larger stone. (see Figure 2-9A.) If we were asked how the man in Figure 2-9A could move a rock many times his own weight, we would say he had good leverage. Very simply this means that the force arm, or the length of the pole from the pivot (called the "fulcrum") to the person applying the force is longer than the resistance arm, that is the length of pole from the fulcrum to the resistance, which is, of course, the rock (see 2-9B).

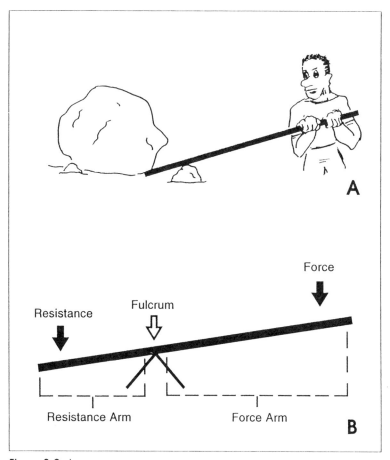

Figure 2-9: Leverage.

Since our bones pivot on each other, they are also levers (see Figures 2-10A and 2-10B) which are moved by the muscles. If you examine human bones, however, you will see that we have very long resistance arms and relatively short force arms. This is because we are not designed for strength but for movement. This fact has a number of implications for the weight trainer. First of all, since we are designed for movement, all exercises should be performed through the entire range of motion. Stretching should be used to maintain flexibility or some of this range of motion can be lost. Secondly, any gains made during weight training will have

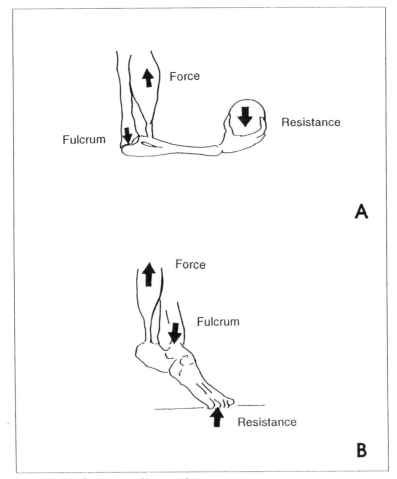

Figure 2-10: Examples of human levers.

a significant impact on performance since the leverage at the joint is usually very poor.

Having looked at the lever systems of the body, we now turn our attention to the types of contractions you can use when you train. There are three types of contractions you need to know.

The first type of contraction is an **isometric** (Figure 2-11A). In this type of contraction, the weight is greater than the force which can be applied by the muscle and therefore the bones cannot move. This lack of movement is the basis of the term *isometric (iso=the same; metric=length)* since the muscle cannot change lengths.

The second type of contraction, the **isotonic** (Figure 2-11B), can be loosely translated as meaning the *same weight.* If you lift a typical barbell or dumbbell, it weighs a certain set amount, and that weight remains constant through the entire range of motion. This has certain implications since you are not equally strong throughout your entire range of motion. In fact, you are much stronger at some joint angles than you are at others. Figure 2-12 (on page 23) illustrates this point by showing the relationship between the angle of the elbow joint and the amount of force which can be produced. As you can see, the arm is strongest when the elbow joint is bent at just less than a 90° angle. This is because the muscle can pull straight up on the bone. The more the arm is straightened, the poorer the angle at which the muscle can pull on the bone and so the weaker you are. This same relationship is true, but to a lesser extent, when your elbow is bent more than 90 percent. Try it out and see for yourself. Since designers of workout equipment recognize this fact, specific devices, called "accommodating resistance" machines, have been designed to improve the lifter's leverage at his or her weakest points and reduce leverage at the strongest points. These machines will be discussed in Chapter 3.

The final type of contraction is **isokinetic** (Figure 2-11C). The term literally means *the same speed.* The machines which provide this type of resistance typically use either a fluid piston or an electromagnet. Many of the newer "high–tech" machines described in Chapter 3 are of this design. In addition, the testing and rehabilitative machines, such as the Biodex and Cybex isokinetic machines, are the ultimate examples of this technology.

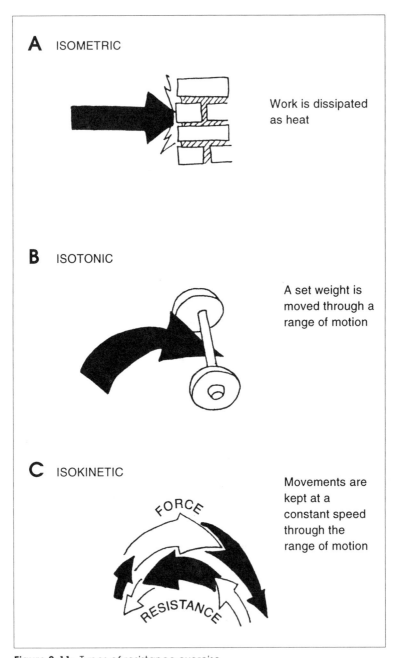

Figure 2-11: Types of resistance exercise.

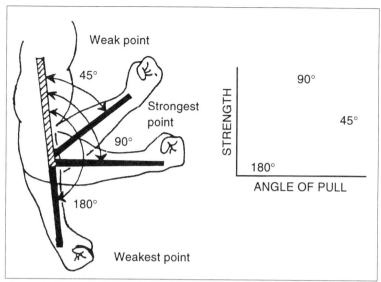

Figure 2-12: The relationship of joint angle to force production for the biceps muscle of the arm.

A FINAL NOTE

Throughout this book, you will be reading very specific information on how an exercise should be done and what changes it will make in the specific muscles of your body. This information is the result of years of research and practical experience in the weight room and is based on the scientific principles reviewed in this chapter. More science will "sneak" into this book as you continue to read. A thorough knowledge of why you are doing a lift a certain way and what modifications in technique you can make to get different results will allow you to tailor your work-out to meet your personal goals. And, when all is said and done, isn't that why you decided to weight train in the first place?

3

Equipment

One of the purposes of this book is to provide a series of weight training exercises which can be practiced either in your home or in the gym. Of course, a minimum amount of equipment is required for any activity but, unlike many sports, there are no recurring costs in weight training once you have access to a basic set of weights.

Since you probably are not yet an Olympic–caliber lifter, you don't have to worry about having the most expensive bar and weights. What you will need can be acquired for approximately $100–$150 and should include the following:

1. A long bar, but lighter than the Olympic bar (barbell).
2. Two short bars (dumbbells).
3. A selection of plastic–covered or metal weights that will fit interchangeably on your bar.
4. A padded bench with stanchions to hold the bar.

Plastic–covered weights are recommended because they allow you to practice more quietly and are much easier on floors. Most beginning weight sets average about 110–120 pounds and, since you can buy additional plates as your strength increases, this should prove more than adequate. If you have a choice between two–and–a–half–pound plates and five–pound plates, purchase the smaller plates since weight can be added more gradually. If you only have five–pound weights and must add two to balance the bar, then you are dealing with an increment of ten pounds. This can become very heavy on some lifts.

Since weight training is based on the concept of progressive resistance, bars with removable plates, rather than nonadjustable dumbbells, are suggested. If nonadjustable weights are purchased, new dumbbells will need to be added for each new strength level.

Figure 3-1 shows the small twenty–pound bar and a flat bench which are usually included in a basic 110–pound weight set. A typical Olympic set, including a flat bench, barbell, and a rack of nonadjustable dumbbells, is shown in Figure 3-2.

FREE WEIGHTS

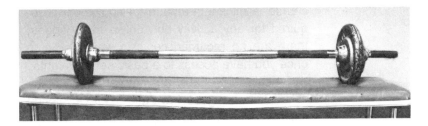

One of the major distinctions between the various pieces of equipment available to the weight trainer is the difference between free weight and machine exercises. Free weights are, very simply, the dumbbells and barbells already described. Free weight exercises are by nature isotonic, since the resistance does not change throughout the range of motion.

The use of free weight exercises has both advantages and disadvantages. The advantages include:

1. **Freedom of movement.** Since free weights are not attached to a track, pulley, lever arm, or belt, weight trainers can vary their movements in all three dimensions throughout the lift. This allows specific targeting of any number of smaller muscle groups by simply modifying certain aspects of the movement.

2. **Limited equipment needs.** The barbells and dumbbells used for one exercise can be used for all exercises. Therefore, the equipment and space requirements are much less for free weights. Basically, they include dumbbell and barbell bars, weight plates, a bench and, if possible, a squat rack and a small workout area.

3. **Development of the accessory muscles.** Since free weights have the potential to move in any of the three planes of motion (see Figure 3-3), it is necessary to control their motion. For example, if a weight is pushed directly up from the shoulders

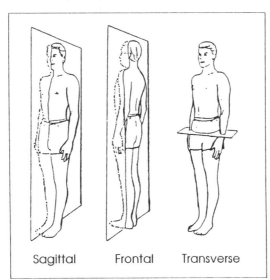

Sagittal   Frontal   Transverse

Figure 3-3: Planes of movement.

(as in the overhead press, Figure 8-6b), it is able to move not only up and down (transverse plane), but forward and backward (frontal plane) and left or right (sagittal plane). Therefore, when weight trainers do the exercise, to keep the weight from drifting forward and backward, they must not only exert force with the prime movers of the shoulder (anterior and medial deltoids) and the arm extensors (triceps brachii), they must also use the muscles of the upper back (posterior deltoids, trapezius, rhomboids) and chest (pectoralis major, pectoralis minor, serratus anterior). To keep the weight from drifting laterally, they must also use the muscles along the sides of the body (latissimus dorsi, teres major, intercostals). Muscles which stabilize the movement are called *accessory muscles,* and they will also be developed during free weight training. When weight machines are examined, you will see that most machines stabilize the weight as they dictate the movement pattern, thus minimizing accessory muscle development.

4. **Balancing development.** When both sides of the body produce force along a dictated movement pattern, sometimes the dominant side of the body performs a greater percentage of the work than does the non–dominant side. For example, a right–handed person might lift more of the weight on a curl machine with the right arm rather than the left. The use of free weights, especially dumbbells, allows the weight trainer to target the weaker muscles and develop better balance. Some machines offer separate movements of each limb (isolateral) and can also provide this benefit.

5. **Speed training for power.** Free weights are also superior for the explosive movements commonly used to develop power. Anyone who has attempted these lifts on pulley or chain–driven machines recognizes that the ballistic nature of the lift causes the weights to bounce, and the chains and cables sometimes disengage, causing the movement to place stresses on both the lifter and the machine—not to mention a disturbing concert of clangs, pings, and whirls. Though not all commercial machines suffer from this limitation, it is a common occurrence with many.

6. **Multi–joint movements.** Some of the most popular lifts used in training programs (for example, the snatch and the power clean, Figure 5-2) require the use of many muscles to move

numerous joints throughout the body. Free weights easily allow these movements, while the limited planes of motion and restrictive nature of machines are not compatible with these lifting techniques.

Although there appear to be few negative aspects to free weight techniques, this is not exactly true. The freedom of movement which makes free weights so beneficial also leads to some of the following problems associated with their use:

1. **Need for spotters.** In most free weight lifts which place the lifter below the weight, a spotter (who watches and helps control the weight) is necessary to reduce the potential for injury. Spotters are especially important during lifts where the individual is under the bar, since the lifter has the potential of being "pinned" by the weights.

2. **Loss of control of weights.** Along with the freedom of movement, which is a benefit of free weights, there is also the potential to lose control of the weights, which may cause injury. Obviously, this possibility is increased with the use of greater weight at the end of a set.

3. **Need to learn proper form.** Unlike machines which guide the weight trainer through the motion, the ability to target specific muscle groups during free weight movements is dependent on maintaining correct form during the lift. This form must be learned and maintained for optimal results.

4. **Maximal resistance is limited by the weakest angle of pull.** As described in Chapter 2, the ability of the muscle to produce force is dependent on the angle of the joint. Therefore, it is impossible for the weight trainer to perform a maximal effort throughout the range of motion using free weights, unless he or she is helped through the weaker points in the range of motion, or "cheats" by not doing the lift using strict form. It is common to see a lifter use "body English" to incorporate other muscles into a lift to "force" a repetition.

5. **It is easier to change weights on machines than it is using free weights.** In order to change weights on a bar it is necessary to remove the restricting collars, remove the weight, put on the new weight, and again replace the collar. This is far more complicated than using machines, since most machines have weight stacks with pins that allow easy and fast selection of the proper weight.

Chapter 8 on free weights will catalogue a number of lifts, describe the major muscle groups and accessory muscles targeted and provide form hints and spotting techniques where appropriate.

Free Weight Accessories

The Incline Bench. The incline bench (Figure 3-4) is used to change the angle of the typical bench press. The change of the angle allows targeting of the upper portion of the chest (upper pectoralis major) and the front area of the shoulders (anterior deltoids). This action is similar to many athletic movements, such as shot–putting and blocking in football, and is helpful in training for strength in these activities. A declined bench, which is reported to target the lower pectoralis area, is also available.

Figure 3-4: The incline bench.

The Squat Rack. The squat rack is extremely helpful for any lift requiring the weight trainer to get under the bar in a standing position. It also provides a resting place for the weight at the end of the exercise. The rack pictured in Figure 3-5 has the added advantage of an inclined plane which will catch the weight should the lifter lose control during the lift. It also provides resting points at various heights for taller and shorter lifters. The squat racks shown in Figures 3-6 and 3-7 are more commonly used, since they provide a similar benefit while requiring less floor space. Some additional uses of the squat rack will be described when more advanced training methods are examined.

Figure 3-5: The squat rack.

Figure 3-6: Squat rack.

Figure 3-7: Squat rack.

The Hack Squat Rack. A typical angled leg press machine, commonly called a hack squat rack, is shown in Figure 3-8. Notice that the lifter is performing a squat along an inclined plane as opposed to moving directly up and down. As can be seen, this machine keeps the weight moving along a set track, allowing the lifter to perform the exercise with a higher level of safety. Of course, this also limits the involvement of the accessory muscles of the shoulders, back and buttocks, which are used to stabilize the body during the free weight squat.

Figure 3-8: Hack squat rack.

The Smith Machine. The Smith machine is illustrated in Figure 3-9. The uprights work as a track to keep the bar in a set plane, while the hook and peg assembly allows the lifter to load the bar with the desired number of plates and, by a simple rotation of the bar, release it to allow the exercise to be performed. Once the work is completed, the bar can be hung at the original level, or lower, should the lifter be unable to complete the final repetition. The Smith machine can be used for the squat, overhead press, and a variety of other exercises.

Figure 3-9: Smith machine.

The Preacher Bench. The preacher bench shown in Figure 3-10 is a padded bench commonly used to isolate the biceps during arm curls. Since this bench restricts the movement of any joint except the elbow, the use of other muscles (such as those of the back, shoulders or legs) is all but eliminated and work is concentrated on the biceps alone.

The E–Z Curl Bar. The E–Z curl bar (see Figure 3-11) is a bar bent specifically to accommodate proper hand and wrist angle during arm curls. Since the hands are forced into a completely flat position using a straight bar, there are additional stresses on the elbow and wrist joints during this exercise. The E–Z curl bar is designed to put the hands in a more compatible anatomical position for both the arm curl and other exercises, such as the

Figure 3-10: Preacher bench.

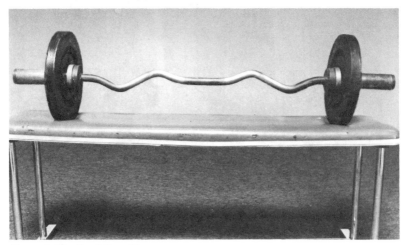

Figure 3-11: The E-Z curl bar.

reverse wrist curl. (see Figures 8-22a and 8-22b) and triceps press. (see Figures 8-19a and 8-19b)

The Toe Raise Machine. Possibly a better description of the toe raise machine (Figure 3-12) is the "heel raise" machine. This machine locks the lower leg into a padded rack so that all the weight must be lifted by pushing up with the foot (raising to your toes). This concentrates the resistance on the calf muscles (gastrocnemius and soleus).

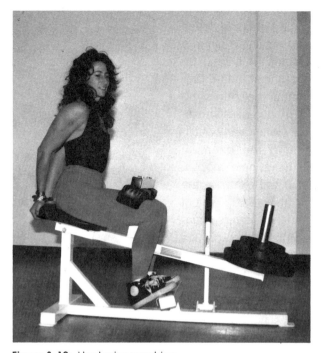

Figure 3-12: Heel raise machine.

While these are not the only accessories you will see in the weight room, they constitute the typical "hard core" devices. There are a number of machines available which provide the same and other benefits as these benches and racks. These machines will be discussed in the next section and in subsequent chapters on lifting techniques.

MACHINES

The large number of machines currently available make it nearly impossible to evaluate the strengths and weaknesses of each. It is possible, however, to consider a number of them as examples of attempts to provide technological answers to the physiological needs of the weight trainer.

The Universal Machine. The Universal machine (Figure 3-13) was probably the earliest and most successful attempt to provide a machine which would be adjustable to a number of weight trainers, provide a safe, controlled environment, isolate specific muscles, and provide ease of changing training loads by simply moving a pin in a weight stack. It should be noted that the standard Universal machine offers no method of adjusting resistance for biomechanical differences in the exercise through the range of motion. Chapter 9 will examine the lifts available to the weight trainer on the Universal machine and the muscle groups which can be selectively targeted using each lift.

Figure 3-13: Universal machine.

Accommodating Resistance

The Nautilus Machine. The Nautilus line was developed by Arthur Jones in the early 1980s. It was the first successful commercial effort to produce a line of accommodating resistance machines. As discussed in Chapter 2, the amount of force which a limb can produce is the result of the muscle pulling on the bone. The angle at which the muscle pulls on the bone directly affects the production of force. Figures 3-14 and 3-15 demonstrate how the Nautilus machine uses a cam and cable system to vary or "accommodate" the resistance to meet the force production of the limb. In the illustration, you can see that the shape of the cam allows a longer lever arm (and therefore more leverage) at the point where the muscle has its poorest angle of pull, and the shortest lever arm (less leverage) where it has its best angle. The desired result is that the machine will give the same desired level of intensity throughout the entire range of motion. This same concept of matching leverage with mechanical differences in force production throughout the range of motion has been incorporated into a number of other machines using similar cams and other lever systems. Chapter 11 will describe a number of the exercises and techniques specific to Nautilus training.

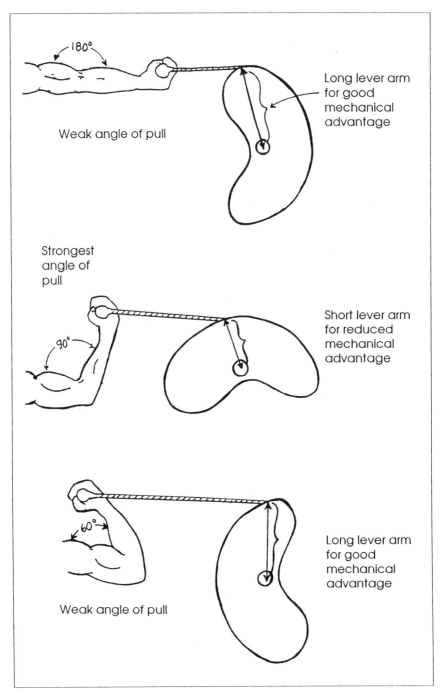

Figure 3-14: Use of a cam to accommodate for biomechanical changes at different joint angles.

Figure 3-15: Cam and cable system.

Isokinetics

Fluid Resistance. A number of machines attempt to simulate true isokinetics by using pistons, similar to automotive shock absorbers, to provide resistance. Since the fluid is forced through a restricted chamber, the faster the individual attempts to move, the greater the resistance to that movement. This condition simulates a true isokinetic exercise, since fluids provide greater friction as the lifter attempts to move the lever arm faster. The degree to which the piston provides restriction to the speed of movement is directly related to the nature of the fluid. Gas–filled pistons are much less restrictive than liquid–filled pistons since gas is compressible. While some of these machines are not truly isokinetic, they are often very successful in their attempt to use physical laws to restrict the speed of motion and provide resistance. The Kaiser line (see Figure 3-16) is probably one of the best examples of this type of machine. This line has the added advantage of allowing the lifter to adjust piston pressure during a session.

Figure 3-16: Piston-type machine.

True Isokinetics (Electromagnetic Resistance). There are a number of machines that allow the user to set specific limits on the exercises. The best known of these machines are made by BIODEX, CYBEX, and KINKOM. They are usually computer–controlled and employ a feedback loop which provides greater resistance as the exerciser attempts to increase speed. Due to their cost and complexity, their use is usually limited to rehabilitation work in a sports medicine facility or hospital. See Figure 3-17.

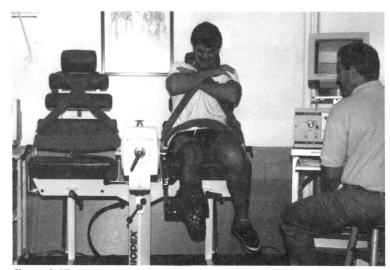

Figure 3-17: Computerized electromagnetic machine.

Hi–Tech Equipment

A number of other machines recently developed use computer technology either in their design or operation.

Hammer lifting equipment, for example, uses a computer-generated, three–dimensional model called "Reggie." The creator of the equipment, Gary Jones, examines the specific needs of athletes and coaches and determines the exact movement patterns necessary to meet these needs. Then, using his computer assisted design (CAD) system, he designs moving lever arms, a seat, and a support frame that are anatomically and biomechanically correct for the movement. The result is a machine with the "feel" of free weights that allows a more comfortable and efficient movement since it follows the same arc–shaped patterns as the human body. Due to the advanced lever arm designs, the impact of the "sticking points" which normally limit free weight movements is minimized. Two such machines, the Isolateral Bench and Isolateral Leg Extension, are shown in Figures 3-18 and 3-19. These machines allow each limb to work independently and use standard weight plates for resistance.

Figure 3-18: Isolateral bench press machine.

Figure 3-19: Isolateral leg extension machine.

The ultimate in high–tech equipment is possibly the new "Life-Circuit" machines. The computerized system which controls these machines provides a number of advantages. First, a preliminary set allows the machine to set up a range of motion and a resistance value based on a desired percentage of the subject's measured 1RM figure. Secondly, the motorized resistance assembly of the machine can be programmed to follow a set lifting pattern and can even provide increased resistance during the negative portion of the movement with no stop in the lift. Add these attributes to a machine that provides feedback concerning the resistance for each set, total weight lifted, number of repetitions and even breaks in form, and you have a picture of the future as the technological revolution enters the world of weight training. The LifeCircuit chest press machine is pictured in Figure 3-20.

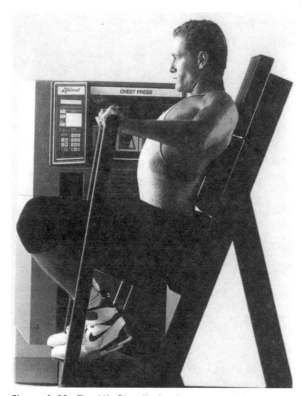

Figure 3-20: The LifeCircuit chest press machine.

Advantages and Disadvantages of Machines

While different machines offer different advantages, some generalizations can be made. The general advantages of machines include:

1. **No need for a spotter.** Since the machine controls the weight and also supports it at the beginning and end of each exercise, no spotter is necessary.

2. **Ease of changing resistance.** In most machines, changing resistance is usually a simple matter of changing a pin, turning a dial, or punching in a digital readout.

3. **No loss of control of the weights.** Since the machine guides the weight, it remains in the proper line of motion throughout the activity.

4. **Optimal weight throughout the range of motion.** Many machines provide methods of maintaining high levels of work throughout the range of motion. This is not possible with free weights.

The disadvantages of machines include:

1. **Cost.** The cost of even the most reasonable machine is far beyond that of free weights, and the cost escalates as the technology improves. There are very few machines within the price range of the individual lifter.

2. **Space requirements are much greater for machines.** Since each exercise generally requires a different machine, floor space to accommodate a full body workout is usually very great.

3. **No accessory muscle development.** Since the weights usually move on tracks by pulleys and chains, there is no need to stabilize the weights by engaging accessory muscles.

4. **Limited number of exercises.** Given the restrictive nature of machines, the subtle changes in hand position or movement pattern possible with free weights are not available on machines.

5. **Speed of movement.** Many machines restrict the speed at which a movement can be made. This sometimes makes faster movements very uncomfortable, thereby limiting speed–specific training.

These advantages and disadvantages are specific to some machines and not others, but all have their benefits and limitations. The best lifting method for you is a matter of your own personal needs and preferences. As you read and gain experience, these needs and preferences will become clear, as will the proper techniques and equipment to meet them. Just remember: as long as you provide proper overload, *all systems will work!*

Fundamental Concepts

As is true of any activity, weight training has its own vocabulary. A knowledge of the terminology will help you to develop and modify your program, and discuss your workout with other weight trainers and coaches. The terms are used to describe movements, training patterns, and lifting techniques.

COMMONLY CONFUSED TERMS

There is a good deal of confusion concerning some very basic terms used to describe physical ability. This should be cleared up before we go any further. Terms such as *strength, power, work,* and *force* are commonly used interchangeably by both the general public and fitness professionals. This confusion leads to real problems when a person attempts to describe his or her specific goals or to quantify the improvements which have been made.

Force is any applied stimulus which can move an object; in weight training this is equal to the weight or "resistance" used during the exercise. **Strength** can best be described as the maximum weight moved or the amount of force exerted by the muscles during a single all–out performance of a specific lift. We often hear people ask "How much can he bench?" or "How much can she squat?" In effect, they are asking how strong that person is. Unfortunately, once this question has been answered, the usual reaction is "Wow, is he or she *powerful!*" These two terms are not the same, however, since **power** is actually the speed at which an individual can produce force. You may often hear coaches talk about an athlete's "explosiveness." This is the same as his or her power. While these differences may not seem important at first, it should be realized that training for strength and training for power require two very different approaches. Later in this chapter, you will see that the difference in lifting technique employed is actually the same as the difference in the definition of the terms, that is, speed of movement. If this difference is not recognized, the weight trainer will never fully attain his or her desired goals.

TRAINING TERMINOLOGY

The **overload principle** states that for a muscle to improve, it must be stressed beyond its normal level of activity. The concept of **specificity of exercise** says that the muscle will **adapt** according to the specific type of overload applied. You should remember that there are **five variables which we can manipulate** in weight training: **intensity, duration, frequency, speed,** and **the specific exercise performed.**

The **intensity** of any lift can be easily manipulated by changing the amount of weight you are lifting. This is important since the strength gains an individual can make are directly related to the amount of weight he or she lifts during a single lifting and lowering of the weight. This single movement is called a **repetition,** or **rep.**

Duration is the length of time an exercise is performed. In weight training, duration is dictated by the number of reps you do (a "set" of reps) as well as the number of sets you perform. For example a typical workout technique might use three **sets** of eight to ten **reps.**

Frequency, very simply, is the number of times you exercise a specific muscle group per week. Numerous studies have shown that the optimal recovery period for a muscle, depending on the severity of the workout, is between 48 and 96 hours. Therefore, most weight trainers will work specific muscle groups every other day. Heavy training performed more frequently than this can lead to progressively greater and greater damage to the muscle fiber and result in overtraining and ultimately, injury.

Speed is generally not included as a separate training variable. It is usually considered to be the intensity component in such training as running, cycling or swimming. It is included as a separate variable in this text since intensity in weight training is most easily defined as the amount of weight lifted.

Thanks to the efforts of strength training coaches, athletes and exercise scientists, the speed component of weight training is receiving more and more attention. It is now recognized that to develop power (explosive strength), it is necessary for a lifter to train at high speeds of contraction.

The last training variable is the **specific exercise performed.** Since certain movements use specific muscle groups, your choice of lifts will allow you to target the exact muscle groups you wish to change. Chapters 8 through 11 will describe these lifts and the muscles they work.

APPLYING THE CONCEPTS

Now that you are familiar with the training variables that can be manipulated and the scientific connection between structure and function, it is time to put the two together so that you can develop an individualized training program. Each person enters the weight room with a picture in his or her mind of the ideal body that he or she wants to develop. All humans have genetic limitations; however, the correct manipulation of the training variables and a regular training program can produce changes that might have at first seemed beyond reach.

Specific Exercises. Certain lifts target specific muscles, and your program should concentrate on developing the muscles you desire to change. Be sure to train both the desired muscle and its antagonist. Too often we become "mirror conscious" when we select our lifts (Figure 4-1); that is to say, we work only the muscles that we see in the mirror. It is not unusual to see individuals doing multiple sets of bench press to develop a mas-sive, muscular chest, and never once doing any rowing exercises to develop the muscles of the back. Such imbalances in training are common and can lead to poor symmetry, and increase the possibility of chronic or acute injury. Remember to concentrate on balance when choosing your lifts.

Figure 4-1: Mirror conscious planning.

Intensity and Duration. Intensity is perhaps the most impor-tant variable for dictating different functional and structural changes in the musculature of the body. As mentioned in Chapter 2, the muscle changes according to the functional demands placed on it. The variable that most precisely dictates these demands is intensity. In fact, **intensity actually dictates the third vari-able, duration.**

Let's examine that statement. The purpose of all weight training is to fail. If you choose to do what is called an eight repetition maximum exercise (8RM), you choose a weight which you can lift eight times and no more. If you can do repetition number nine, you don't have enough weight (a great enough **intensity**) to do a true 8RM set. And, in fact, if you choose a training routine where you plan to do three sets of eight repetitions and you succeed at doing all three sets, your intensity is too low and you should raise your weight—this is the practical application of progressive resistance.

Consider the impact various training intensities and durations can have on the specific adaptations made by the muscle. It must be realized that the figures given here are very general. In addition, they do not reflect the cyclic changes usually prescribed for athletes as they progress through a competitive season. These considerations and other specialized topics will be covered elsewhere in the book.

It is generally agreed that lifts in the 3-5RM range are most efficient for the development of strength, 7-12RM for increasing muscle mass, and 15RM or more for muscular endurance. The number of sets to be used, however, is far less defined. There is little doubt that multiple sets are necessary to produce maximal gains in both strength and size. Some guidelines have been set by scientific research and practical experience. For example, a minimum of three sets appears to be necessary for significant increases in strength and size to occur. It is not unusual, however, to see strength coaches employing as many as five or six sets during strength and power training. Even greater extremes are often used by bodybuilders. Since there appears to be a significant correlation between the volume of work performed and the resulting increase in the size of the muscle, these lifters often perform as many as 20 sets of seven to twelve repetitions in an attempt to maximize their size gains.

Your decision should be based on what you wish to accomplish and the amount of time you feel you can dedicate to your training. The most common guideline followed by the recreational lifter is three sets of eight to twelve reps for each muscle group targeted. This pattern has been shown to be effective in promoting significant gains in both strength and size. In addition, both the number of sets and the weight can be adjusted to target certain muscle groups and promote specific changes.

Speed. The manipulation of speed is now receiving greater attention, thanks to the interest among the athletic community in developing power. Many universities are using high speed lifts to train their power athletes in the belief that such specific speed training will promote not only strength, but also the speed of contraction necessary to maximize power production.

On the subject of speed, it is interesting to note that a number of studies have shown that slow, deliberate movements promote the greatest increases in the size of the muscle. It appears to be especially important to emphasize the eccentric (negative) portion of the lift to promote maximal growth. It is for this reason that we find the bodybuilding community working at these reduced rates of speed. As you can see from this single comparison, the muscle will make very different changes when exposed to something as simple as differences in speed. Therefore, you should develop a clear picture of the goals you wish to attain before you begin your program.

Frequency. Finally, the frequency of training is an important consideration since weight training is a significant stress to the muscle, and it requires time for the tissue damage resulting from a training bout to be repaired. As stated earlier, 48 hours is the most commonly used recovery interval between workouts; however, longer rest intervals may be necessary if high–intensity and high–volume work are used.

INITIAL CONSIDERATIONS

It has been shown that the muscle is able to increase its force production long before the muscle or connective tissue can thicken to a sufficient degree to handle the increased tension. This has been attributed to an improved ability of the nervous system to fire the muscle. Therefore, it is recommended that you begin your lifting program with light weights and work up slowly over the first three to four weeks. One rule of thumb is to establish a 20RM figure and do a typical 8-12RM workout using this reduced load. Then gradually increase the load until it reflects a true 8-12RM.

Since you will be aware of your increased strength very quickly, you will be tempted to increase weight much too soon. If you allow yourself to fall into this trap, you can expect the following scenario:
1. A sense of great pride and accomplishment after the workout is completed.
2. Some minor soreness which may limit your range of motion approximately two or three hours following the workout. This soreness is usually concentrated near the tendons where the muscle tissue is thinnest and most vulnerable to injury.

3. Extreme soreness by the next morning, which will make it very painful to move the joint and nearly impossible to fully extend or flex the affected arm or leg. This condition is called DOMS (delayed onset of muscle soreness) and in cases of extreme overwork, can become so painful that the affected area will be impossible to move and will even begin to develop localized swelling (edema).

4. Continued pain for approximately a week, which will make further training impossible unless you intend to begin the entire pain cycle again and create sufficient damage to push training back even further.

Depending on the severity of the damage, this mistake can easily delay your training far beyond the initial time you would have spent slowly increasing your weight and will be much more painful.

GETTING STARTED

Once you have gradually increased your weight to the actual target figure you have selected, it is time to begin your lifting program. The program itself should include a number of important aspects:

First, the program should be carefully planned and written out so that an exact pattern can be followed. This will give you a template to follow and prevent the confusion that often occurs as you attempt to remember exercises, loads and repetition figures; and, it will allow you to map your progress and make the increases in resistance necessary for further improvement.

Second, an adequate warm–up should be used. A general warm–up of approximately five to ten minutes is appropriate. It should consist of low–intensity activities such as light calisthenics, stationary cycling, light jogging or any activity to increase the heart rate, blood flow and body temperature. This general warm–up will prepare the body for exercise by increasing delivery of oxygen, nutrients and appropriate hormones, but even more important, it will decrease the viscosity (make it more pliable) of the muscle and connective tissue.

Muscle, and to a lesser degree connective tissue, can be compared to gelatin. If you put gelatin in the freezer you can break it, splinter it, and chop it. In the refrigerator it becomes a rubber–

like mass that stretches considerably before it breaks. Taken out of the refrigerator and placed on the counter, the longer it stays at room temperature, the softer and more liquid it becomes, until it is very much like water. Muscle and connective tissue also become more fluid at high body temperatures, and therefore much more resistant to damage than when they are cold. This is very important in a high–intensity activity such as weight training.

This warming up of the muscle is so important that each exercise you perform should include a warm–up set, at a low resistance, to allow for an increase in localized heat and blood flow to the muscle to be exercised.

Third, be sure to stretch before and after each workout. Chapter 6 will discuss the variations in stretching techniques and the particular stretches that will target specific muscle groups.

Fourth, perform all exercises under control and through the full range of motion. This statement is often misinterpreted so that control is defined as slow, deliberate movements. It should be recognized that the speed of movement can be varied according to the goals of your training; however, the weights should not be thrown or allowed to move outside of the desired movement pattern. Remember, loss of control of the weights can lead to severe injury. In addition, if exercises are not done throughout the entire range of motion, a loss of flexibility can result.

Fifth, exercise the larger muscle groups first. This will allow you to concentrate on the smaller groups using less weight and with better control. This provides optimal resistance during the later exercises and reduces the chance of injury since these lower weights will be more easily controlled by the fatigued muscles.

Sixth, be sure to balance your workout by exercising opposing muscle groups either on the same day or on alternate days. This is important for both symmetry and balance.

And as a final safety consideration, unless spotters are present, do not perform the bench press or other lifts in which you may be pinned if control is lost. However, if you do decide to bench press alone, do not use collars so that weights can be tilted off in an emergency.

A BREATH OF FRESH AIR

When lifting, it is very important to control your breathing. Whenever a muscle is contracted, the tension within that muscle causes a momentary reduction in blood flow. This might be compared to stepping on a garden hose while water is flowing through it. Not only would the flow of water be reduced, but the pressure within the hose would increase. This same increase in pressure occurs in the blood vessels of your working muscles. The degree of blockage (or occlusion) increases with the weight of the lift and is nearly complete at 70 percent of your maximum and above. This is normal and does not become a problem unless you combine lifting extremely heavy weights with holding your breath. Breath–holding increases the pressure within the chest, where the large blood vessels and heart are located and adds additional pressure. When breath–holding and heavy lifting are combined, blood pressure can become extremely high and then drop tremendously as the resistance is released between reps.

These extreme changes in pressure are dangerous since they can cause minor damage to the blood vessels during the contraction, and dizziness and loss of equilibrium as each rep is completed. Although this situation does reflect an extreme condition, it is recommended that you exhale during the positive (concentric) portion of the lift and inhale during the eccentric (negative) portion. This simple practice will reduce your risk to nearly zero.

5

Establishing Your Program

Now that you understand the scientific principles of building muscle, are familiar with the equipment and understand the fundamentals, let's plan your program.

Humans have vastly different ideas of what they want and like. Automobiles are delivered in hundreds of colors, restaurant menus have pages filled with different foods, and clothing catalogues are often so large that they require a well–trained individual just to lift them. The first step in establishing your program is to decide what *you* want to accomplish.

To assist you, we have designed two charts. They work much like a menu in a Chinese restaurant. Just pick your muscles from Chart A, and combine them with the goals from Chart B, and you will have an individualized program.

Chart A: The Master Muscle Chart. Chart A is simple to use. Pick the muscle you want to work, look it up on the chart, and find the exercise for that muscle. Look up the exercise in Chapters 9, 10, and 11, and you are ready to go. If you don't know the name of the muscle you want to work, Appendix C has a full muscle chart to help you find it.

Exercises by Muscle Group and Equipment

	Free weights	Multi-station equipment	Nautilus equipment
Neck group	Isometric contractions of the neck	Neck harness	4-way neck Rotary neck Neck and shoulder
Deltoids	Overhead press Lateral raise Front raise Inclined bench press	Overhead press	Overhead press Lateral raise
Trapezius	Shoulder shrug Upright row Bent lateral raise Bent-over row Single arm row High arm curl	Shoulder shrug	Neck and shoulder Rowing torso

Pectoralis majors	Bench press (inclined and flat)
	Dumbbell fly (inclined and flat)
		Bench press
		Parallel
			Double chest
			  1. arm cross
			  2. decline
			Parallel dip on multi-exercise

Biceps	Front barbell curl Reverse curl Preacher curl	Curl Chin	Compound curl Biceps curl Multi curl
Triceps	Triceps extension French press	Press down	Triceps extension

continued...

	Free weights	Multi-station equipment	Nautilus equipment
Forearm group	Wrist curl (straight, reverse, or pronated)	Wrist curl	Wrist curl on multi-exercise
Latissimus dorsi	Supine overhead dumbbell raise Bent-over row Chin-ups	Chin-up Pulldown on lat machine	Pullover Behind neck Torso/arm Chin-up on multi-exercise
Abdominal and oblique group	Sit-up Crunches Cross crunches	Sit-up Leg raise	Abdominal Rotary torso Side bend on multi-exercise
Obliques	Side bends Twists Cross crunches	Side bends	Side bends
Gluteal and erector spinae group	Squat Stiff-legged deadlift Forward bends	Leg press Hyperextension	Hip and back Hip abduction Leg press
Quadriceps	Squat Lunges	Leg extension Leg press	Leg extension Leg press
Hamstrings	Squat Lunges Side kicks	Leg curl Leg press	Leg curl Leg press
Abductor group	Squat	Leg press	Hip abduction
Gasrocnemius and soleus group	Toe raise	Toe press	Calf raise on multi-exercise Toe press on leg press

Chart B: The Personal Options Chart. Of course, Chart A is only part of your program development. To fully meet your personal needs, you must now use Chart B. It presents some options concerning the way you want to change your body. Each option contains beginning and advanced techniques which have proven to be successful in achieving the goals you have chosen. Select the technique and then read the details in the remainder of the chapter. You should recognize that all techniques will give some benefit in all the options, but the ones given under a particular category serve to optimize the benefits in the chosen option. For example, significant strength gains may be realized using a system designed to increase bulk, and a slight increase in strength will result from an aerobic lifting program. What you must realize is that each system recommended is designed to maximize your selected goal, and the more dissimilar the goals, the less one goal will contribute to the successful attainment of another.

GOALS	BASIC				ADVANCED
	RM	Sets	Speed (positive-negative)	Rest	
General Toning	8-12	3	2-4 sec.	2-3 min.	
Strength	3-6	5	2-4 sec.	2-3 min.	Pyramid System, Split Program, Functional Isometric
Bulk (Muscle Mass)	6-12	3-10	2-4 sec.	2-3 min.	Super Sets, Split Program, Blitz System, Functional Isometrics Pyramid System
Power (Speed)	3-8	5	max - controlled speed	2-3 min.	Olympic Lifts, High Speed Concentric Only System, Power Lifts, Functional Isometrics
Aerobic Conditioning (Weight Loss)	10-15	3	2-4 sec.	15-30 sec.	Circuit Training, Super Circuit
Local Muscle Endurance	20-30	3	2-4 sec.	2-3 min.	Progressive Fatigue System, Declining Reps System

Chart B: Personal Options Chart

SYSTEMS

Pyramid System. This system starts with a high repetition figure (low weight) and progressively drops the number of reps to a maximum (1RM), then increases the number of sets to the original high repetition figure. Figure 5-1 illustrates the technique graphically. This system can be modified by doing only the rising or falling leg of the pyramid.

This system is reported by its proponents to be one of the best ways to increase strength. Bodybuilders often use this technique to increase bulk.

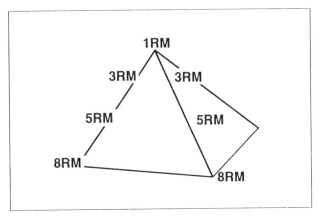

Figure 5-1: Pyramid System.

Split Program. Since maximal increases in bulk require both high–intensity and high–volume training, the potential for muscle damage and the need for recovery are very important. As stated earlier, optimal recovery is believed to take about 48 hours; therefore, many lifters use a split program. This means the lifter alternates the muscles exercised on different days. There are a number of systems such as:

Push–Pull: Alternate days when pressing or extension exercises (pushes) are done with days when curling or flexing exercises (pulls) are done.

Upper Body–Lower Body: Alternate a day which concentrates on the arms, chest, neck, and upper back with a day which concentrates on the abdominal, lower back, quads, hamstrings and calves.

Agonist–Antagonist: Alternate the muscles on one side of each joint with those on the other side on alternating days.

These systems are not the only systems possible, but they serve as an example of how workouts can be split to allow lifting to occur every day.

Functional Isometrics. Since all lifts have a point at which the lifter is at a poor biomechanical position, the lifter often requires help to get past this point and complete the lift. This point is often called the "sticking point" of the lift. It has long been known that isometric training builds strength at the point where it is performed, but creates little improvement elsewhere. Functional isometrics makes use of both these ideas by having the lifter push at maximal force against an immovable object at his or her "sticking point." This training will allow the lifter to push greater weight through the "sticking point" and thus increase the load during the entire exercise.

Super Sets. Super sets are probably the most frequently discussed aspects of advanced training methods. The system usually involves multiple sets of different exercises all designed to overload the same muscle groups. The sets are usually performed at a 6-15RM figure moving quickly from one exercise to another. For example, a military press might be followed by an inclined bench and lateral raise to superset the shoulders. The intensity of this type of training can be increased even further by super setting the antagonist muscle.

Blitz System. The blitz system is well–named. In this system, the lifter concentrates on a single body part in each daily session. As you begin to frequent lifting gyms, you'll hear many serious weight trainers, especially bodybuilders, say things like, "I do arms on Monday." or "Tuesday is my leg day." Typically, you may find that the lifter will do between eight and fifteen sets of eight to twelve repetitions using three or more exercises per muscle group. This system is designed to place maximum emphasis on a body part and then maximize the rest period. You should realize that this technique puts extreme stress on each body part and should not be used by the beginning lifter.

Olympic and Modified Olympic Lifts. There are two lifts used in Olympic competition: the clean and jerk and the snatch. Both lifts are done at maximal speed, since the competitor's ability to "get under the bar" quickly often separates success from failure. Figure 5-2 presents each lift being performed. Since the clean and jerk constitutes two separate motions, strength coaches often take this lift apart and do each section separately. "Power cleans," for example, are now an integral part of nearly every power athlete's training program. The power clean is illustrated in Chapter 8 on free weights. The typical 3-5RM figure is used for three to five sets. One word of caution: these multiple joint lifts done at high speed carry a high potential for injury if done incorrectly. We advise that a weight trainer obtain professional coaching from a certified coach before attempting them.

The power clean.　　The snatch.

Figure 5-2.

High Speed Concentric Only System. This system was developed for swimmers. The lifter performs the concentric portion of the lift as quickly as possible, and the weight is allowed to "drop" (controlled release with minimal contraction) during the eccentric phase. Three to five sets of 10 to 20 reps are used. This type of training attempts to target only the functional muscle, while it increases the power across a more endurance based time frame. Although scientific research confirming its success is lacking, the concept seems worth examining.

Power Lifting. Power lifting, by definition, is high speed lifting. The lifts incorporated in competition are the squat, deadlift and bench press. To develop power, athletes are instructed to "explode" from the starting position throughout the concentric portion of the lift. As with all power training, low RM figures are used. The same precautions should be observed in this type of training as with Olympic and modified Olympic lifts: get sound instruction before attempting them, and remember they are for the advanced lifter, not the novice.

Circuit Training. Although weight training is not normally thought of as an aerobic exercise, it is possible to increase the aerobic benefit of the workout by increasing the RM figure (which of course means decreasing weight), and reducing the rest interval between sets. This is the aim of circuit training. An aerobic circuit uses an 8-15RM figure. When lifters complete one muscle group, they move quickly (within 15 to 30 seconds) to another group, repeating this pattern until all muscle groups are completed (usually 10 to 12 exercises). This type of training can significantly increase aerobic capacity, but not to the extent possible with distance training or aerobic interval training. The system does produce the added benefit of increasing both muscle mass and strength to a much greater degree than running, aerobic dance or other cardiovascular activities.

Super Circuit. This system employs the same techniques as circuit training with a slightly longer interval between lifts (approximately one minute). During this interval, the lifter does not rest, but rather switches to an aerobic or muscle endurance activity such as sit–ups, stationary jogging, stationary cycling, stepping, or any other aerobic activity to keep the heart rate elevated throughout the workout. This type of training is extremely challenging, and not recommended for the beginner.

Progressive Fatigue System. This system employs a high number of repetitions (20 to 25) per set. The lifter starts with a 25RM figure and then progressively lowers the weight until he or she can no longer complete the necessary number of reps for each successive set. Rest intervals will range from 30 seconds to two minutes depending on the desired intensity of the workout. The number of sets can also be increased as the lifter becomes better trained. It would be reasonable for the experienced lifter or endurance athlete to begin with three sets which would provide a minimum of 60 to 75 total repetitions per body part. As you continue to lift, you will establish the weights necessary to maximize each set.

Declining Rep System. This system is similar to the Progressive Fatigue System. However, in this system, the weight lifted remains unchanged, and the weight trainer attempts to do the maximum number of reps possible. Rest intervals are again kept short and the workout begins at a 20-25RM. The number of sets completed depends on the individual, but a minimum of three is recommended.

The systems presented above do not constitute all those currently in use. With a knowledge of the relationships between the physiology of change and exercise choice you may manipulate the variables in ways to suit your needs, and even develop your own modifications of these systems.

Summary. Once you have chosen one of these systems, you should examine the routine and try to understand why it works. If you cannot understand the reasoning behind a system, you may wish to review the previous chapters. Once you can understand the reasons, you will have the ability to evaluate the many systems other lifters will recommend in the gym and decide if they have any factual basis. This ability will not only keep you from wasting valuable workout time, it may also prevent the injuries that often accompany poorly planned programs.

6

Stretching and Flexibility

This chapter is of special interest to the weight trainer. Some "facts" about stretching and flexibility are really myths that have developed over the years. It is necessary to seperate the myths from the facts. To begin, we will explain the term flexibility.

Defining flexibility is somewhat like defining life, we all know it when we see it; but if someone asks for an exact definition, it requires considerable thought, and many of the definitions are either too complex or incomplete. Let's keep our definition as simple as possible. Flexibility is the range of motion of a joint. To understand this, use your arm. Hold it out in front of your body, palm up, and straighten it as much as you can. Notice that it locks out and is limited by the structure of the bones, connective tissue, and muscles. Now bend your elbow and flex it as far as possible. Again it is stopped; but this time, it is stopped by the muscles of the forearm hitting the biceps. This is the range of motion of your arm.

THE MYTH OF THE "MUSCLE-BOUND"

Since we're talking about range of motion, let's discuss the best-known myth in weight training: becoming "muscle bound." The term itself conveys a picture of a person with so much muscle that he can't scratch his own back. For years, this picture had been associated with weight training. Many coaches refused to weight train their athletes, because they believed they would become inflexible, slow and unable to perform. Many physicians avoided weight training during rehabilitation, because they were afraid their patients would "bulk up" and be unable to make natural movements. The public echoed these opinions as if they were absolute truths carved in stone.

Current research, however, shows a completely different relationship between weight training and flexibility. Exercise physiologists have shown that flexibility can not only be maintained, it can actually be increased by the use of proper weight training techniques using full range of motion exercises. While most studies indicate that there is no loss in flexibility due to resistance training, we ask the reader to remember one very obvious fact: when those biceps and forearms get bigger and bump into each other as you flex your arm, your arm stops. This is obviously a loss in range of motion. However, it has nothing to do with the physiological limits of the tissues, and everything to do with a simple law of physics: two objects cannot exist in the same place at the same time.

COMPONENTS OF FLEXIBILITY

There are two basic components of flexibility: first, the mechanical limitations caused by the muscle and connective tissue; and second, the protective mechanisms, which the nervous system uses to prevent muscle injury. Although each of these components is handled separately, they work together in defining the flexibility of any joint.

The Mechanical Component. The mechanical limitations caused by the muscle and connective tissue have been further divided into what are called the series and parallel elastic components. Very simply, these are the protein structures that connect the parts of the muscle to each other (series) and wrap or surround the muscle (parallel) and can be stretched (elastic). Figure 6-1 illustrates this principal.

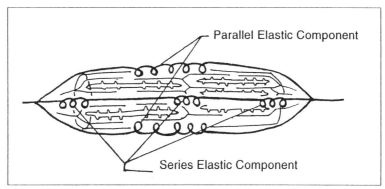

Parallel Elastic Component

Series Elastic Component

Figure 6-1: Mechanical components of flexibility.

The Neural Component. The protective mechanisms of the nervous system are called reflexes. If you close your eyes and move your arm, you know exactly where it is without looking, because your body has "receptors" or sensors that can "feel" the movement and tell you the arm's position. These receptors also provide a line of defense designed to prevent injury. Since this defense must happen quickly, it doesn't go through your brain. It happens by a simple loop of nerves that run from your muscle to your spinal cord, and back to your muscle. This is called a spinal reflex. We're all familiar with the simple knee jerk reflex: when the doctor taps your knee with a rubber mallet, you kick. This is the stretch reflex and is sensed by receptors called muscle spindles, which are buried within the muscle parallel to the fibers (see Figure 6-2). When your muscle is stretched quickly (also called ballistically), the spindles feel the stretch and send a message back to the muscle to contract, so that the stretch won't go too far and injure the muscle or joint.

A second reflex is the inverse–stretch reflex and is sensed by a completely different receptor located in the muscle tendon. This is called the Golgi Tendon Organ and it senses when the tendon is overly stretched. These receptors are in series with the muscle and require a much higher level of tension before they are activated. For this reason, we will consider the stretch reflex (muscle spindle) only in our discussion.

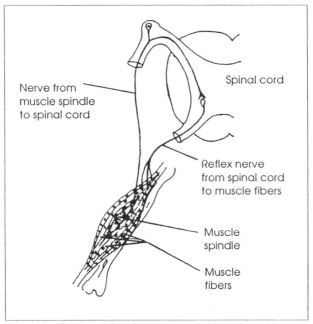

Figure 6-2: The stretch reflex

How To Stretch

The mechanical limitations of muscle and connective tissue are the result of the interaction of the elastic and resistive properties of the tissues. When you begin to think about stretching, think about this comparison: your muscles, tendons and ligaments are like taffy. If you put it in the freezer, it gets hard as a rock; but if you leave it in the car on a hot day, you can stretch it to five or ten times its length without it breaking. When stretching, **get the muscle and connective tissue warm**.

The neural component is equally important, since a fast ballistic movement will cause an opposing contraction by the muscle (stretch reflex), while a slow movement will allow the muscle spin-dles time to reset themselves with each increase in length, and thereby reduce the intensity of the stretch reflex. Given these two scenarios, we can now prescribe a basic technique for stretching.

The need to warm the tissues indicates that the lifter should perform a light workout such as calisthenics, bicycling, brisk walking, or jogging at about 50 percent of his or her maximum heart rate before stretching. Maximum heart rate is estimated by taking 220 and subtracting your age. This should last between five and ten minutes so that the lifter can feel an elevation in body temperature, a "general warm–up." Following this, each joint that is to be worked during the session should be slowly and gently stretched without undue discomfort. Each stretch should be held for 20 to 30 seconds and repeated at least twice. Many lifters perform a light warm–up set before each lift to increase the temperature of the specific muscles and joints involved in that lift.

When To Stretch

At the very least, you should stretch before and after each workout. Remember, this is as much a part of your workout as the lifts. Nearly everyone who exercises, whether they be lifters, runners, tennis players, or any other competitive or recreational athlete, fails to stretch sufficiently. When we are fatigued, we leave out the stretching. When we are short of time, we leave out the stretching. When we describe our workout, we leave out the stretching. Unfortunately, the only time we tend to think about stretching is after an injury or loss of flexibility, which could have been prevented by...stretching. So every time you work out, *warm–up, cool down,* and *stretch.* And if you are at home, stretch while you're listening to music, watching television or reading— there's always time.

An Added Benefit Of Lifting

While it is true that incorrect lifting may cause a loss of flexibility, it is also true that correct lifting methods can actually increase flexibility. Research has shown that performing exercises through the full range of motion and concentrating on a slow eccentric movement can cause significant increases in the flexibility of the lifter. This is likely due to the increased tension put on the fibers during the lowering of a weight. Since studies examining the electrical activity of the muscle have shown that fewer fibers are activated during the eccentric (lengthening) movement, each fiber develops more tension, and therefore is stretched further during this portion of the lift.

SPECIFICITY OF STRETCHING

Lifters should recognize that just as specific lifts target different muscles and connective tissues, specific stretches do the same. Therefore, we have included in this book a number of common stretches which are designed to target specific areas and safely allow the individual to increase his or her flexibility.

Upper Body Stretches

Exercise: Static Neck Stretches (Figure 6-3).
Areas: The cervical spine and neck musculature.
Procedure: Gently lower the chin to the chest, stretching the back of the neck. Point the chin toward the ceiling, stretching the front of the neck. Try to lay the ear on one shoulder and then the other, stretching the sides of the neck. Then try to put the chin in each armpit, stretching the neck on an angled plane. Hold each stretch for the prescribed 20–30 seconds. **Do not rotate the neck while stretching, this stresses the cervical spine.**

Figure 6-3a.   **Figure 6-3b.**   **Figure 6-3c.**

Note that the intensity of this stretch can be increased by using the arm to increase the tension on the muscles, as in Figure 6-4.

Figure 6-4.

Figure 6-5.

Exercise: Cross–armed Rotator Cuff Stretch (Figure 6-5).
Areas: Side and front of the deltoids (shoulders).
Procedures: Sit upright with your right arm bent at 90 degrees. Reach across and under with your left arm and grab your right wrist. Apply pressure outward. Switch arms and repeat the exercise.

Figure 6-6.

Exercise: Cross–body Shoulder Stretch (Figure 6-6).
Areas: Side and back of the deltoids.
Procedures: Reach over your right shoulder with your left hand. Grasp your left elbow with your right hand and apply pressure backward and to the right. Switch arms and repeat the exercise.

Figure 6-7.

Exercise: Behind the Back Cross–body Shoulder Stretch (Figure 6-7).
Areas: Side and front of the deltoids.
Procedures: Reach behind your back with your left arm. Grab your left elbow with your right hand. Pull gently across the body. Switch arms and repeat the exercise.

Exercise: Doorway Stretch (Figure 6-8).

Areas: Front of the deltoids and pectoralis (chest).

Procedures: Stand in a doorway with upper arm at shoulder height or slightly higher. Place the forearms on each side of the doorway and gently step and lean through.

Figure 6-8.

Exercise: Shoulder Stretch with a Partner (Figure 6-9).

Areas: Front of the deltoids and pectoralis (chest).

Procedures: With your palms down, raise your arms up from your side to a position level with the floor. Have your partner push your arms toward the middle of your body. Figure 6-10 shows an alternate method that maintains the arms at a higher level.

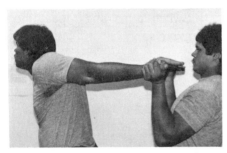

Figure 6-9.

Figure 6-10.

Exercise: Triceps Stretch (Figure 6-11).

Areas: Triceps (back of upper arm).

Procedures: Point your right elbow toward the ceiling and drop your arm down your back. Grasp the elbow with your left hand and apply pressure down, back and toward the midline of the body. Switch sides and repeat the exercise. Figure 6-12 shows a partner aiding in the performance.

Figure 6-11.   Figure 6-12.

Lower Body Stretches

Exercise: Cat Stretches (6-13 and 6-14).

Areas: Lower back.

Procedures: Get down on your hands and knees. Arch your back by trying to touch the back of your head to your buttocks. Then arch your back upward (chin toward thighs). Hold this position as you slowly sit back on your heels.

Figure 6-13.

Figure 6-14a.   **Figure 6-14b.**

Exercise: Twisting Stretch (Figure 6-15).

Areas: Waist rotators and lower back.

Procedures: Place your right leg over your left with the knee bent to about 90 degrees. Put your left elbow behind the knee. Rotate, using the elbow for leverage. Change sides and repeat the exercise.

Figure 6-15.

Exercise: Knee Crossovers (6-16).

Areas: Waist rotators and lower back.

Procedures: Lie on your back and bring your left knee to your stomach. Grasp the knee with your right hand and pull it across your body. To increase the intensity of this stretch, try it with the leg straight (Figure 6-17).

Figure 6-16.

Figure 6-17a.

Figure 6-17b.

Exercise: Lateral Straddle Stretch (Figure 6-18).

Areas: Hamstrings and lower back.

Procedures: Sitting erect on the floor, extend your right leg and tuck your left foot into your groin area with the foot against the inner right thigh. Bend forward at the waist and attempt to touch your chest to the right thigh. Change sides and repeat the exercise. This exercise can also be performed using a towel (6-19), or with a partner to add intensity (6-20).

Figure 6-18.

Figure 6-19.

Figure 6-20.

Exercise: Standing Quadriceps Stretch (Figure 6-21).

Areas: Front of the thigh (Quadriceps).

Procedures: Stand upright, leaning against a stationary object for balance. Bring your right foot up toward your buttocks. Grasp right ankle in your left hand and pull it up and toward the leg. Change sides and repeat the exercise.

Figure 6-21.

Exercise: Seated Leg Stretch (Figure 6-22).

Areas: Hip extensors and buttocks.

Procedures: Sit upright, extend the left leg, flex the right leg, and bring it toward your chest. Grab the right ankle with your left hand, and block the leg with your right forearm and elbow. Pull the foot toward the left shoulder. Change sides and repeat the exercise.

Figure 6-22.

Exercise: Back Lotus (Figure 6-23).

Areas: Groin and Hips.

Procedures: Lie on your back, knees bent, so that the soles of the feet are together. Let the knees go slowly toward the floor. You may increase intensity by gently pushing on the inner thighs.

Figure 6-23.

Exercise: Butterfly Stretch (Figure 6-24).

Areas: Groin and Hips.

Procedures: Sit with the knees bent and the soles of the feet touching. Grasp your ankles to hold the feet together and apply gentle pressure to the inner thigh, forcing the knees toward the floor. The intensity of this stretch can be increased by using the help of a partner (Figure 6-25).

Figure 6-24.   **Figure 6-25.**

Exercise: Standing Calf Stretch (Figure 6-26).

Areas: Calf muscles (gastrocnemius and soleus).

Procedures: Stand facing the wall and place your hands slightly above and wider than the shoulders. Bring the right foot back until you have trouble keeping it on the ground. Now push forward slowly, controlling the tension with your arms. If the knee is locked, this will stretch the gastrocnemius (Figure 6-26a). If bent, the soleus receives the majority of the tension (Figure 6-26b).

Figure 6-26a.   **Figure 6-26b.**

SUMMARY

Although the previous exercises do not cover all possible stretching techniques, they do provide a thorough, static routine for the muscles commonly involved in strength training. For a more complete examination of the topic, including assisted methods such as Proprioceptive Neural Facilitation (PNF), the reader is directed toward texts that concentrate specifically on stretching and flexibility.

Dietary Considerations for the Weight Trainer

The subject of sports nutrition is too complex to cover in a weight training text. However, it may be helpful for the beginning lifter to examine some of the critical aspects of caloric intake, protein requirements, vitamins and supplements. In addition, a brief discussion of ergogenic aids (performance enhancing substances) should be of interest.

BODY WEIGHT: THE FIRST CONSIDERATION

Although this chapter concerns nutrition and diet, these two subjects cannot be discussed without some background information concerning body composition. The human body is made up of a number of different tissues. The most important ones are muscle, bone, and fat. Muscle and bone are the two components that make up what we call lean body mass (LBM). Fat is considered by itself. If we take an individual and place his or her fat weight over body weight, we come up with a very important number, the body fat percentage. Let's give two examples. A 160-pound man who is found to have 40 pounds of fat and

130 pounds LBM, and a 220-pound man with 44 pounds of fat and 180 pounds LBM. If we compute the percentage of body fat for each, we get:

$$\%BF \text{ (160 lb. man)} = (40 \text{ lb. fat}/160 \text{ lb. LBM}) \times 100$$
$$\%BF = 25\%$$
$$\%BF \text{ (220 lb. man)} = (44 \text{ lb. fat}/220 \text{ lb. LBM}) \times 100$$
$$\%BF = 20\%$$

As you can see, even though the 220-pound man has four pounds more body fat, his overall percentage of body fat is lower. This point is made for two very important reasons. First, many people measure their success or failure in a weight lifting program by how much weight they lose or gain. As you can see from the example above, the important thing is not how much weight you lose or gain, it is the *type* of weight you lose or gain. As you continue to lift, you may either gain weight or remain the same. People who are slightly overweight often consider this as a sign of failure. But if you realize that lifting increases your muscle and bone mass, remaining the same or gaining may very well be due to a gain in LBM which is actually reducing your percent of body fat.

The second important point is that the use of ideal weight charts, such as those used by insurance companies, is not appropriate for the individual engaged in weight training. When doing body composition evaluations, it is not uncommon to find a 158-pound man who comes out at a perfect weight on the ideal weight chart for his 5'11" height, but due to his inactive lifestyle has a very low LBM and is 27 or 28 percent body fat. We then evaluate a 5'11" athlete who weighs 200 pounds and is therefore considered 42 pounds overweight by the same ideal weight chart, but because 168 pounds of his weight are bone and muscle, his body fat is only 12 percent.

In short, the body weight of an individual, while an indicator of fitness, is not to be considered of great importance, especially in the person who is weight training.

HOW TO ASSESS BODY FAT

There are a number of methods used to assess body fat. The highest standard at this time is underwater weighing (see Figure 7-1). Using this procedure, an individual's exact percentage of

Figure 7-1: Underwater weighing.

body fat and LBM can be computed. This can be done because fat is less dense than water (it floats), while muscle and bone are more dense than water (they sink). This being the case, we can use a formula which compares a person's weight on land compared to his or her weight in the water to get a very accurate evaluation of body fat percentage. You can probably find an underwater weighing station if you contact the physical education or sports science department of most universities.

There are a number of other methods which are currently used. One is a local measurement of body fat thickness using a device called a skin caliper (see Figure 7-2). Although this form of measurement provides a reliable estimate of the individual's percent body fat, the estimate is only as

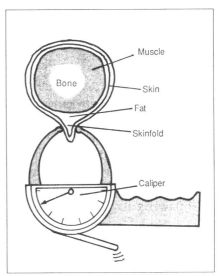

Figure 7-2: A skinfold caliper measures the amount of fat between two layers of skin.

good as the method used and the individual doing the measuring. Each formula has been developed for a specific age group and/or sex, and if the wrong formula is used, incorrect measurements are produced. It has also been our experience that variations as great as 8 to 10 percent are seen among different technicians due to poor skills, incorrect angles of measurement, and incorrect measurement sites. Be sure that these variables are considered if you are evaluated using this technique.

Two newly available techniques are electrical impedance and infrared evaluations. Each provides a fairly accurate evaluation; however, each has its flaws. No doubt, with further experimentation these methods will prove very accurate, but at this time it is suggested that their use be accompanied by one of the more proven methods (especially underwater weighing) to confirm the results.

CALORIES IN—CALORIES OUT

One of the first questions a beginning lifter asks is: "What should I eat?" This question really contains a number of lesser questions. How much should I eat? What foods should I eat? How much of each food should I eat? What do I need besides a normal diet to improve my muscle function or gain muscle mass?

Let's start with the first question. How much should I eat? The exact answer is impossible without a complex evaluation of your individual metabolic function, but it is possible for the weight trainer to closely estimate the correct number of calories he or she requires, and then check the accuracy of the estimate by changes in body weight and body composition.

The first step in making this estimate is to compute the resting (or basal) metabolic rate (BMR) of the individual. This computation is different for men and women. It is also based on weight and age. You must remember, however, if you are an individual with a high percentage of body fat, the calculation may be somewhat higher than normal. If this is the case, we suggest you use your LBM + 15 percent for males and + 20 percent for females. Then do the following computation:

Males   —   (Body weight in lbs./2.2) x 24
Females —   (Body weight in lbs./2.2) x 21.6

An example of the calculation for a 180–pound male is as follows:

180/2.2 x 24 = 1968 calories

This is the minimal number of calories a 180–pound male would need to sustain bodily functions. Any activity above this will require that he use stored body fuels such as fat, or the stored muscle sugar called glycogen.

The next computation should be your activity cost. Again, this is computed according to your body weight. A conservative estimate of the caloric requirements of a student over a normal day would be approximately 6 calories/pound of body weight/day. Given the same 180–pound student:

$$6 \times 180 \quad = \quad 1{,}080 \text{ calories}$$
$$\text{adding the BMR} \quad = \quad \underline{1{,}968 \text{ calories}}$$
$$\text{for a total of } 3{,}048 \text{ calories/day}$$

If we then add the estimated caloric cost of an hour of resistance training at .04 calories/pound body weight/minute and assuming an active lifting time of 30 minutes weight training = .04 x 180 x 30 = 216 + 3,048 = 3,264 calories. For each decade of life past thirty years of age, it would be appropriate to reduce this requirement by approximately 10 percent due to a reduced BMR.

This figure is slightly lower than the *Encyclopedia of Sports Science and Medicine* estimate of 4,650 calories per day required for competitive weight lifters; however, that estimate is based on competitive athletes rather than individuals who are weight training.

How Much Of What?

The human body uses three basic fuels: carbohydrates, fats, and protein. The first thing every beginning weight trainer learns is that muscle is made of protein, and therefore, he or she must take in sufficient protein to allow muscle growth. Unfortunately, the second thing the new lifter often does is increase his or her protein intake far beyond the actual requirements.

What are the actual requirements? The United States Food and Drug Administration recommends .8 grams/kg body weight/day. If we again examine our 180–pound student, the computations are as follows:

180 lbs./2.2 lbs./kg x .8 gram = 65.5 grams

However, recent studies on body builders and weight trainers have shown that this amount is insufficient to allow increased muscle mass. Newer estimates recommend approximately 1.8 grams/kg body weight/day.

> 180/2.2 x 1.8 = 147.3 grams

This is a maximal figure. Increasing the protein content above this amount will provide the lifter with no additional muscle mass, and actually will force the kidneys to work harder to clear waste products due to the increased protein.

To put the protein figure in perspective, let's look at a few dishes you might eat. A half–pound serving of fish contains approximately 65 grams of protein, a typical hamburger contains 25 grams of protein, and a small steak may have as much as 23 grams of protein. In short, if you read the labels of what you eat, you will find that the standard American diet easily provides sufficient protein to stimulate muscle growth.

Additional Foods

Most sports scientists and nutritionists agree that the active individual's diet should consist of 60 to 75 percent carbohydrates, and most of these should be complex carbohydrates such as cereals, pasta, potatoes and other starches. Since carbohydrates provide approximately 4 calories/gram, another simple computation will allow you to compute your carbohydrate intake:

> Grams of carbohydrate = (Your caloric allowance x .7)/4

> calories/gram

Again using our 180–pound student, you will recall that his caloric allowance was a healthy 3,259 calories. Therefore, the computation would be:

> (3264 x .7) / 4 = 571 grams or 2,285 calories

We can put this carbohydrate value in perspective using some examples:

1 APPLE	=	23 GRAMS
1 BANANA	=	27 GRAMS
1 CUP OF RAISINS	=	115 GRAMS
1 BOWL OF SPAGHETTI (4 cups)	=	140 GRAMS

Taking these two energy sources we then have:

Total calories	3,264
— Calories from carbohydrate	2,285
Total	979
— Calories from protein	735
Total calories from fat	244

Using a value of 8 calories/gram of fat, this allows approximately 30 grams of fat in the diet. You will find that this is very little fat since much of what we eat contains fat. Therefore, you should be very careful about your fat intake. For example, that hamburger with 25 grams of protein probably had at least 10 grams of fat, but the fish which contained 65 grams of protein only had 5 grams of fat. Most vegetables and fruits have little or no fat. In addition, remember that reducing the carbohydrate content by five percent can increase your fat allowance by 20 grams.

For The Potential Vegetarian

Since vegetables and fruits have such a low fat content and still contain substantial carbohydrates and protein, a vegetarian diet may seem like a feasible alternative to the lifter. However, vegetable protein is not complete and cannot be used to build muscle unless the proper mix of vegetables is used. If you are considering such a diet, we suggest that you first consult with a dietician or study a good text which deals with proper methods.

Vitamins And Supplements

For most of us, the necessary vitamins and supplements are already contained in the foods we eat and it is a mistake to believe that more is better. Just as excess protein needs to be eliminated in the urine, the same is true of most vitamins and minerals.

Vitamins are not food and they cannot be substituted for meals. They are chemicals that allow us to effectively use the food we eat. Minerals serve the same purpose, in addition to being used in building bone structure. If you wish to ensure that you are receiving a proper level of vitamins and minerals, you can take a multi-vitamin. This will probably supply more vitamins and minerals than you actually need, a sort of "nutritional insurance policy."

There is no need to spend big bucks on natural vitamin sources. The body cannot tell the difference. To your body, vitamin C is vitamin C whether it comes from the lab or an orange. So eat well, and if you feel it is necessary, take a multi–vitamin.

One additional note on supplementation for the female lifters: if you are considering a multi–vitamin, it would be advisable to take one with additional iron and calcium. Also, be sure that it contains the FDA recommended allowances of Vitamin D.

DRINKING AND THIRST

If you are working hard, you will probably lose a considerable amount of water through perspiration. You will also lose salts (called electrolytes) which are necessary for muscle contraction. Since the duration of your lifting session will probably be less than two hours, there is no need to replace electrolytes, since there is not a noticeable loss of salt during such short workouts.

You should, however, replace the lost fluid. Probably the best plan of attack is to hydrate before you begin your workout. A good start is sixteen ounces of water. Then replace approximately 4–6 ounces of water every 15 to 20 minutes. The best bet is very cold water. Don't be afraid of cold water; it does not cause cramps, and it is absorbed by your body more quickly than warmer water.

If you would like to use sports drinks such as Gatorade®, Excell®, or other similar products, they will do you no harm, but they have been shown to be of little benefit in short exercise bouts under the controlled temperature conditions in which you will probably be lifting.

WHAT ABOUT STEROIDS?

Steroids belong to a group of chemicals called ergogenic aids which are sometimes taken by athletes to improve performance. Although they have been shown to work, the long–range side–effects of steroids are so extreme that the gains they produce are not worth the risks. The side effects in females include:

• larger appetite—reversible.
• decreased breast size—partially reversible.
• less body fat—reversible.
• increased sex drive—partially reversible.

- increased sex drive—partially reversible.
- increased body hair—partially reversible.
- clitoral enlargement—non–reversible.
- behavioral changes—reversible.
- acne—reversible.

The changes that can't be observed are probably the most dangerous and include:

- decreased high density lipoprotein (HDL: the good fat carrier in the blood) and increased low density lipoprotein (LDL: the bad fat carrier in the blood).
- high blood pressure.
- liver cancer and other degenerative diseases of the liver.
- decreased female sex hormones.

In males, there have been deaths. Impotency is also a common occurrence as well as male pattern baldness which is non–reversible.

SUMMARY

In summary, the weight trainer should eat a healthy, balanced diet high in complex carbohydrates and with sufficient, but not excessive, protein. Fat intake should be kept as low as possible. A multi–vitamin can be used if you feel it necessary to ensure proper vitamin and mineral levels, and you should drink fluids regularly while you lift to reduce the risk of dehydration and improve your performance.

And, finally, stay away from steroids and other ergogenic aids, they were developed for medical use by doctors, and using them for building muscles is not only inappropriate it is extremely dangerous.

Chapter

8

Free Weight Lifts

ISOMETRIC CONTRACTIONS OF THE NECK

Erector spinae, sternocleido-mastoid, superior fibers of the trapezius

Although there are a number of machines and weighted headgear that can be used to strengthen the neck there are few accessory–free exercises. The wrestlers bridge is often recommended, but due to its potential to cause injury—especially in the beginning lifter, its use is not recommended. Instead, we have included a series of isometric exercises that isolate the front, back and each side of the neck. When coupled with the other exercises that work the trapezius and posterior deltoids, sufficient size and strength can be achieved. Figures 8-1a through 8-1d illustrate exercises you can do alone. The idea is to apply sufficient pressure to the front, back or side of the neck so that you can push as hard as possible without moving your neck. The pressure and the contraction should be applied gradually (one to two seconds) and held for a count of approximately 10 to 15 seconds.

89

Figure 8-1a.

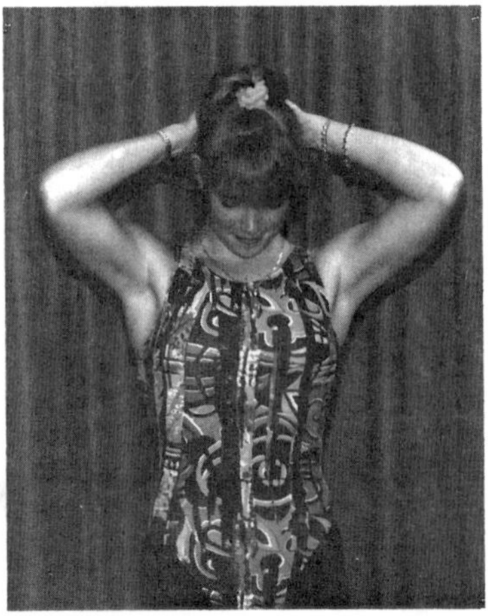

Figure 8-1b.

Figure 8-1c.

Figure 8-1d.

If a partner is available, a towel can be used to apply the resistance and you can concentrate solely on the contraction. Again, be sure the pressure is applied gradually. If you are the partner, you should only apply sufficient pressure to resist movement. Figures 8-2a through 8-2d show these techniques.

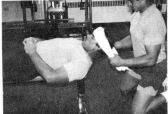

Figure 8-2a.   Figure 8-2b.

Figure 8-2c.   Figure 8-2d.

SHOULDERS AND NECK

Upright Row
Deltoids, upper trapezius, sternocleidomastoid, biceps, radialis

The upright row is an excellent lift for upper back and shoulder development. To begin, grasp the bar palms down with the hands close together. Stand straight and rest the bar against the front of the thigh. Now pull the bar to your chin and try to keep your elbows as high as possible. Remember that this close grip makes it more difficult to control the bar so be sure to concentrate on keeping it level throughout the range of motion. See Figures 8-3a and 8-3b.

Figure 8-3a.   Figure 8-3b.

Shoulder Shrug
Upper trapezius, deltoids, radialis, biceps,
sternocleidomastoid

The shoulder shrug is one of the simplest and best exercises for targeting the muscles of the upper back. The exercise is pictured in Figures 8-4a and 8-4b. To perform the exercise, stand erect, hold the barbell or two dumbbells at arm's length and try to shrug your shoulders as if you are trying to touch them to your ears. Try to avoid the common mistake of using too much weight. You should be able to do this exercise through the full range of motion. If you want to check this, do a few shrugs without the weight so that you can "feel" the range of the movement before adding resistance.

Figure 8-4a.   **Figure 8-4b.**

Bent Lateral Raises
Posterior deltoids, rhomboids, and trapezius

One of the problems with most upper body exercises is that the front and sides of the deltoids are usually worked quite well, but the rear part at the back of the shoulders may receive little or no attention. The bent lateral raise not only works this portion of the deltoids, it also provides an excellent workout for the two muscles between the shoulder blades, the trapezius and rhomboids.

To achieve the desired effect, you should lean forward to an angle of about 50-80 degrees. Now, keeping your arms nearly straight, raise a pair of dumbbells to the sides as high as you can and return them to their original position. The intensity of the exercise can be varied during a set by bending the arms to a lesser or greater degree. See Figures 8-5a and 8-5b for an illustration of the technique.

Figure 8-5a.

Figure 8-5b.

Overhead Press
Deltoids and triceps

The overhead press is one of the most effective means of developing the front portion of the deltoid muscles.

To begin, bend the knees and grasp the bar with an overhand grip (knuckles facing away) with the hands a little wider than your shoulders. Stand and bring the bar to a thigh rest position. Then bend elbows and snap the bar to a position where it will be resting on the palms at chest level. A slight knee dip will allow you to better bring your hips under the bar and will cushion the impact of the bar when it comes to rest against the upper chest (Figure 8-6a).

At this point, thrust the hips slightly forward, tensing thighs, buttocks, and low back muscles as you push the weighted bar smoothly overhead. The bar should pass close to your face and then directly overhead (Figure 8-6b). Remember to take a breath before pressing the weights upward, exhale as the arms straighten, and inhale as you lower to begin another rep.

Since this exercise is the first in a series of "pinned" exercises, where the lifter is under the bar, we have included a spotter in the illustrations. Note that the spotter is present to help the lifter if he or she is too fatigued to complete the movement. Should it become necessary (in an extreme case) to escape the lift, the bar should be pushed forward away from the body as both the lifter and spotter step back.

Figure 8-6a.   **Figure 8-6b.**

A simple variation of this lift is the sitting press. As with any of the pinned exercises in this text, we have again included a spotter in the illustrations (Figures 8-7a and 8-7b). Note that the spotter is in a position where he can assist with the lift by applying the necessary force just near the triceps, or can take the bar should the lifter be unable to maintain control. Since this variation of the lift uses a behind–the–neck technique, the spotter also has the additional task of handing the bar to the lifter and replacing it in the rack when the lift is completed. This behind–the–neck position provides more stress on the posterior fibers of the deltoids. Begin this lift with the bar overhead and lower it until it lightly touches your neck. As soon as it touches, push the weight up to arms' length. Be sure to control the weight, especially during the eccentric (lowering) portion of the lift to prevent injury to the neck.

Figure 8-7a.

Figure 8-7b.

Lateral Raises

Deltoids

The lateral raise is an excellent exercise for developing the sides of your shoulders. Because you should keep your arms almost straight, it will be very difficult to do this exercise with heavy weights. It is especially important with this exercise that you do not sacrifice form for the sake of ego. Your muscles will be better served by good form than heavy weights. We have included a spotter in the pictures for this exercise also. While this is not a pinned exercise, the position of the weights relative to the body makes them hard to control and the "sticking points," which prevent the completion of the exercise, are extremely difficult to move through. Therefore, the spotter can help the lifter control the weights and work past the sticking points so that he can benefit from the rest of the movement, especially the extremely important eccentric phase.

To perform the exercise, stand with your arms at your side, palms facing inward, with a dumbbell in each hand. Bend the knees and back slightly for comfort. Now raise both dumbbells to the side, keeping the arms as straight as possible without locking out the elbows. Raise the weights to slightly above shoulder level then lower them to prepare for the next repetition. This is illustrated in Figures 8-8a and 8-8b.

Figure 8-8a.   **Figure 8-8b.**

Front Raise
Anterior (front) deltoids

To begin this lift, stand tall, with the weight in your lifting hand. Raise one arm at time. The arm should be bent slightly during the lift, the weight should be kept away from the body for added intensity. Fist and elbow should raise to chin height and on a level plane. Be sure arms are kept extended on the lowering phase. Figures 8-9a and 8-9b illustrate the beginning and end points of the lift.

Figure 8-9a.   **Figure 8-9b.**

SHOULDERS AND CHEST

Inclined Press

Anterior (front) deltoids, upper fibers of the
pectoralis major, triceps, serratus anterior

The inclined press is an excellent exercise for the upper chest
and front of the shoulders, as well as those little half–moon–
shaped cuts in the rib area formed by the muscles called the
serratus anterior. Since this exercise combines a pinned position
with the added problem of controlling the bar, a spotter is almost
a necessity. The spotter can take a position behind the inclined
bench (the better benches provide a spotter's platform), and can
provide help by placing his or her hands slightly inside or outside
the lifter's grip, depending on its width and the position of the
upright racks. The common method of spotting with the knuckles
forward and a narrow grip in the center of the bar is not recommended, since the grip does not allow the spotter to stabilize the
bar, nor does it provide the necessary position to handle the weight
should the lifter fail completely.

Figures 8-10a and 8-10b show this exercise. To perform it, look
up, take the weight from the rack and hold it directly above the
eyes. Then slowly lower the bar, allowing it to take a slightly
forward path to the upper part of the chest. At this point, drive the
weight back up by pushing with the chest and shoulders and
straightening the elbows.

Figure 8-10a.

Figure 8-10b.

One final precaution, with any bench press there is always a
hidden, or sometimes not so hidden, desire to show off your
strength. This is often attempted by lifting more weight than you

can handle and forcing it up by twisting or arching the body. This can also lead to serious injuries which may greatly delay your training, depending on the degree of injury.

Inclined Fly
Anterior (front) deltoids, upper fibers of the pectoralis major, serratus anterior

This exercise is a variation of the barbell press and is an excellent means of working the shoulders and arms equally. It also is an excellent way to firm the chest area above the bust.

To perform the exercise, lie back on the inclined bench with two dumbbells that you can adequately handle (see Figure 8-11a). Now push the weights towards the ceiling, trying to fully extend the arms. To completely work all muscles involved, try to extend as shown in the pictures, but also extend so that the dumbbells are pointing toward your ears when the arms are fully locked. (See Figure 8-11b.)

Figure 8-11a.   Figure 8-11b.

CHEST AND ARMS

Barbell Bench Press
Pectorals, deltoids, triceps

The bench press is extremely effective for the development of strength and muscle size for the chest, shoulders, and arms. However, this is one of the most dangerous pinning lifts. Remember that if you are too fatigued to finish a repetition, the weighted bar is going to come down, and most likely it will be across your upper chest or throat. A few people have lost their lives doing this exercise, so it is critical that you exercise good judgment concerning the desired weight and that you use a spotter during heavy lifts.

To begin, lie face up on an exercise bench with your knees bent, your feet flat on the floor, and your buttocks and shoulder blades in contact with the bench. Lift the barbell from the rack above the eyes in an arms–extended position. See Figure 8-12a.

Now lower the barbell to the chest, pause momentarily, and recover to the starting position (Figure 8-12b). The spotter should assist the lifter into the starting position. If the lifter is unable to complete a repetition, the spotter should assist only as much as is needed to complete the movement. The lifter will most likely need assistance when the bar is at the sticking position near the chest, but the spotter should be alert to the lifter's condition throughout the movement. The spotter should be bent at the waist with the hands under the bar.

Figure 8-12a.

Note: Since this is an exercise where the sticking point is critical to the completion of the lift, functional isometrics are often used to overcome this area of weakness. The reader is directed to Chapter 5, page 60 for more information on this technique.

Figure 8-12b.

Flat Dumbbell Fly
Pectoralis, serratus anterior, and intercostals (rib muscles)

This exercise is an excellent isolation exercise for defining the musculature of the chest. In addition, although it is not possible to increase bust size, it is possible to effectively improve the appearance of the bust by firming and strengthening the pectoralis muscle of the chest, making this a desirable exercise for women who wish to maintain a high bust line.

To begin, take a supine (lying on back) position on a bench. Hold a dumbbell in each hand, straight up over the chest with palms pointing inward. Slowly lower the weights, trying to keep the arms straight. Be careful to keep the weights parallel since this produces the best effect. When you have lowered the weights as far as possible, slowly bring the weights to their original position. The lift will be improved if you try to squeeze the chest muscles together as you lift. Also, the flexibility of this area, which is difficult to stretch, will be improved during the eccentric movement the further you lower the weights. See Figures 8-13a and 8-13b.

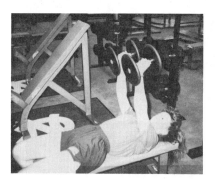

Figure 8-13a.   Figure 8-13b.

UPPER ARMS

Front Barbell Curl
This is the traditional "show me your muscle" exercise, and the best way to perform it follows. Assume a comfortable stance with

the bar resting across the thighs. You should have an underhand grip (palms pointing forward at hip width), then slowly flex your arms, bringing the bar to your chest. Take special care to prevent the elbows from moving backward. Also, try to keep from leaning backward and swinging the weights to chest level. Remember to lower the bar slowly and to fully extend the elbows before repeating the movement. This, more than any exercise, lends itself to cheating. A traditional series of beginner's mistakes are to chose too heavy a weight, rock the hips back and get the elbows behind the body, then drive the hips forward and throw the bar up to its top position. This series of mistakes is further compounded by dropping the bar instead of lowering it slowly. Except for training you to be good at throwing a bar with your hips and bruising your thighs, this serves no purpose at all. See Figures 8-14a and 8-14b for the correct form.

Figure 8-14a.   Figure 8-14b.

Reverse Curl

Biceps, radialis, brachioradialis, wrist flexors

The reverse curl is performed in the same manner as the front curl except the palms are turned forward rather than backward. Reverse curls work the extensors of the forearms very strongly and because of this, you will probably be able to handle less weight than in the front curl. You will note that the lifter in Figures 8-15a and 8-15b is using an E–Z curl bar to improve wrist position.

Figure 8-15a.   Figure 8-15b.

Preacher Curls

Biceps, radialis, brachioradialis, wrist flexors or extensors

Preacher curls work the same muscle groups as the two previous exercises. The advantage of using a preacher's bench is that the arm muscles are isolated by the bench, which blocks the body from being involved in the exercise. This process ensures that the full intensity of the exercise is concentrated on the arm musculature. A lifter using this bench is shown in Figures 8-16a and 8-16b.

Figure 8-16a.   Figure 8-16b.

Single Arm Concentration Curls

When a preacher's bench is not available, or when you desire to work arms independently, a dumbbell may be used for single arm isolation curls. Begin by placing one elbow firmly against your leg (See Figure 8-17a). Now flex the arm, taking care to maintain arm–elbow contact with your leg at all times (See Figure 8-17b).

Figure 8-17a.   **Figure 8-17b.**

Triceps Extension
Triceps

This simple exercise is one of the best isolation lifts for the rear musculature of the upper arm. To begin, lift a dumbbell above your head, keeping your elbow in close to your head. Then reach across behind your neck with the opposite arm and grasp the outer side of the arm to be exercised. The arm placed behind the head will serve two important purposes: (1) it will keep the elbow in and therefore, maintain the correct position for isolation of the triceps; and (2) it will allow you to act as your own spotter by preventing you from bouncing the weight off the back of your head and by giving you an additional hand to help with the completion of a rep which you might not have finished otherwise. Once this hand is in position, bend your elbow very slowly, lowering the weighted hand behind your head until the weights touch your back. Still keeping the elbow in close to your head, straighten the arm, returning the dumbbell to its original overhead position. See Figures 8-18a and 8-18b for an illustration of the technique.

Figure 8-18a.   Figure 8-18b.

French Press
Triceps

This form of triceps extension is commonly called a French press or triceps press. It is also an excellent exercise for strengthening and firming the back or under portion of the arm. One word of caution: do not use excessive weight during this exercise, since it has a reputation for causing sore elbows, and some people may find that their bodies cannot adapt to this particular stress.

To begin, place your hands about 8-12 inches apart and press a light barbell over your head. Keeping your elbows as close together as possible, lower the weight behind your head.

Try to keep the elbows perpendicular or straight up, using them as a hinge for the movement. See Figures 8-19a and 8-19b.

A variation of this exercise is often performed by lying flat on a bench, extending the weight overhead and then lowering it as described above.

Figure 8-19a.   Figure 8-19b.

FOREARM, WRIST AND FINGERS

Wrist Curls
Wrist flexors of the forearm

Almost all sports rely heavily on forearm, wrist and finger strength. Begin the exercise by picking the barbell or dumbbells up with an underhand grip with the hands less than shoulder–width apart. Sit on a bench and extend the hands beyond the knees with the forearms supported on your thighs. Now raise and lower the weight by moving hands, wrists, and fingers only. One word of caution: if you do the exercise too fast, the bar may roll past the fingertips and hit the floor. See Figures 8-20a and 8-20b.

Figure 8-20a.

Figure 8-20b.

This exercise can also be performed using dumbbells if you desire to isolate one arm from the other in an attempt to balance symmetry or strength. This technique is shown in Figures 8-21a and 8-21b.

Figure 8-21a.   **Figure 8-21b.**

The Reverse Wrist Curl

This exercise uses an overhand grip, with the thumbs toward the center of the bar and the knuckles pointing up and away. As you can see from this movement, it works the extensor muscles of the forearm. As with the wrist curl, this exercise prevents the biceps muscles from aiding in the lift and forces a greater effort from the forearm musculature. See Figures 8-22a and 8-22b.

Figure 8-22a.

Figure 8-22b.

Pronated Wrist Curls

This is an excellent exercise for a person who plays a racquet sport because it stresses the wrist muscles in the so–called "hammer position." To begin, grasp the dumbbell at one extreme end and allow it to point downward toward the floor. Now slowly raise the lower end until it is pointing almost directly upward. Figures 8-23a and 8-23b illustrate the exercise.

Figure 8-23a.

Figure 8-23b.

UPPER BACK

Bent Over Barbell Row
Trapezius, rhomboids, biceps

This exercise is designed to isolate the muscles of the upper back, which bring the shoulder blades (scapulae) closer together. When performing the exercise, you should maintain a slight bend at the knee, keep your head up, and flatten or slightly bow your lower back. To perform the exercise, stand over the bar and bend at the knees and waist. Using a wide overhand (palms down) grip, grasp the bar and lift it from the ground, allowing the arms to hang straight. Maintaining an angle of approximately 50 to 80 degrees at the waist, pull the bar into your chest by drawing the shoulder blades together. Then return the bar to the hanging position. Be sure to keep the head up and use a weight you can control, since the back is in a somewhat vulnerable position during this lift. Figures 8-24a and 8-24b show the exercise.

Figure 8-24a.   Figure 8-24b.

Single Arm Row
Trapezius, rhomboids, biceps, and obliques

This exercise works the same muscles as the bent over row; however, it allows isolation on a single side and provides a greater degree of support for the lower back muscles.

Begin by grasping the dumbbell in your right hand and place your left foot just a little forward of your right. Then bend forward until the upper part of your body is nearly parallel to the floor. Use your free hand to hold on to something for balance, or place the elbow across your left knee for a stabilizing effect. The right arm and shoulder should be pointing straight down beneath you to the floor. See Figure 8-25a.

Pull the weight upward to the right side of the chest by raising the shoulder and slightly rotating the torso. See Figure 8-25b.

Pause at the top of the lift, then lower the weight, rotating the torso back into its original position with the arm and weight pointed toward the floor. After fatiguing the right arm, switch to the left.

Figure 8-25a.   **Figure 8-25b.**

High Arm Curl
Trapezius, rhomboids, biceps, posterior deltoids, and obliques

The high arm curl is another excellent exercise for the upper back, arm and posterior shoulder muscles. To begin, assume a bent lunge position (Figure 8-26a) with the weight close to the forward foot. Now pull the weight almost straight up as in Figure 8-26b until it is as high as you can lift it without turning the hand over and pressing overhead. See Figure 8-26c.

Figure 8-26a.   **Figure 8-26b.**   **Figure 8-26c.**

Supine Overhead Dumbbell Raise
Latissimus dorsi, teres major, serratus anterior, intercostals

Normally the lats and the other related muscle groups used during this exercise are easily targeted by using the lat pulldown exercise shown in Chapter 9 on the Universal Machine. However, when such a cable and pulley system is not available, the supine overhead dumbbell raise can be used.

To perform the exercise, get a dumbbell and lie on your back on a flat bench. Taking the dumbbell in both hands, hold it at arms' length directly above your chest. Now, slowly reach back toward the head of the bench, keeping your arms as straight as possible. Lower the weight as far as possible or just before contact with the floor, then raise it back upward to the starting position. Once again, there is the added benefit of an excellent stretch when this exercise is performed through the full range of motion. Pictures of the exercise are shown in Figures 8-27a and 8-27b.

Figure 8-27a.

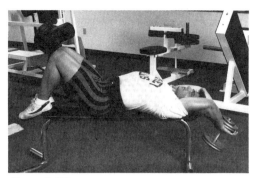

Figure 8-27b.

Chin–Ups

Latissimus dorsi, rhomboids, biceps, finger flexors

Chinning is another excellent exercise for the latissimus dorsi muscles and, to a lesser extent, is beneficial for the entire upper torso.

However, do not be discouraged if you are not able to do as many repetitions as you would like to. Simply hanging and struggling upward will provide a beginning toward the development of these muscles.

As your strength increases, assume a wider grip on the bar with your hands as this will increase the resistance. Additional resistance also may be added by hanging a weight from a belt around your waist. See Figures 8-28a and 8-28b.

Figure 8-28a.   **Figure 8-28b.**

ABDOMINALS

Sit-Ups

Abdominals, quadriceps, hip flexors

The best exercise for the front abdominals is the exercise that people have probably done the most—the old fashioned sit-up. However, there are some variations which will enable you to increase the resistance, and target the muscles (the obliques) which twist the torso at the waist. We'll discuss these next, but first let's describe how to perform the basic sit-up correctly.

Lie on a flat surface with knees bent and feet moderately close to the buttocks. We recommend this position since there have been some indications that straight leg sit-ups can put undue stress on the lower back musculature. The arms and hands should be folded across the chest. We recommend this position instead of the behind-the-neck position to protect the neck from injury. When we are fatigued and attempting a forced sit-up, most of us pull ourselves through the movement by placing pressure on the back of the neck. The cross-chest hand position will avoid this problem. Keeping the abdominals contracted, curl your body through the entire motion to a full sitting position, then lower it until your shoulder blades touch the floor.

You should note that in Figures 8-29a, 8-29b, and 8-29c, the individual doing the sit-up has her feet under a long bar. This allows the hip flexors to take a more active part in the exercise. The same exercise can be done with no holding point for the feet, thereby raising the intensity on the abdominals.

Remember to keep your lower back as flat on the floor as possible; don't raise and lower your hips or do the movement quickly in an attempt to throw yourself through the exercise; and think of the sit-up as curling your body up, rather than lifting your upper body with your abdominal muscles. Finally, remember there are no exercises which allow you to target fat and remove it from a specific area, and this includes sit-ups. All these exercises can do is strengthen and tone the muscle under the fat. So watch your diet, work out regularly, and you'll be able to show off those firm abdominals.

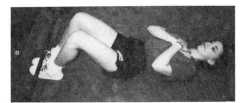

Figure 8-29a.

Figure 8-29b.

Figure 8-29c.

Abdominal Crunches

Abdominals, hip flexors, and quadriceps

The crunch is the latest craze in abdominal exercises. Simply described, it is a sit–up which has been shortened to a limited range of motion, never allowing the abdominals to relax throughout the movement. This produces the burn characteristic of other exercises, such as partial arm curls, which utilize the same technique. The reason for this burn is that when a muscle is held in constant tension, the pressure of its contraction prevents sufficient blood flow to the area (see Chapter 2). This, in turn, prevents the washout of waste products such as lactic acid from the muscles causing the discomfort we call a burn. The benefits, if any, of a burn are questionable, so think of this exercise as beneficial not because it hurts, but because it targets and intensely works the abdominals.

To perform the exercise, take the same position as described in the sit–up, and perform the same movement. In this case, however, when you curl upward, stop the movement as soon as the lower portion of you shoulder blades lose contact with the floor and never allow you upper body to go back down to a flat, resting position on the floor. Figures 8-30a and 8-30b show the first and last positions in the movement.

Figure 8-30a.

Figure 8-30b.

Cross Crunches
Obliques, abdominals, hip flexors, and quadriceps

The cross crunch is another high–intensity, isolation exercise for the waist area. Its main purpose is to target the rotator muscles of the waist called the obliques. These muscles wrap the waist like a shawl, and if you remember our discussion on structure and function, this wrapping around the waist means that when the muscle on either side of the waist contracts, it will rotate the body.

The exercise is begun in the same position as the sit–up or crunch. However, in this case, the ankle of one leg is placed on the knee of the other so that the lower leg is parallel to the ground (see Figure 8-31a). Now, the exerciser attempts to touch the knee with the opposite elbow by curling up and twisting the torso (see Figure 8-31b). As with the standard crunch, the individual should stop when the right shoulder blade leaves the floor, and never relax by lying back completely.

Figure 8-31a.

Figure 8-31b.

HIPS AND WAIST

Side Bends
Lateral flexors, erector spinae, abdominals

This is a very simple but effective exercise designed to firm waist, hips and abdominals.

To begin, stand tall with a dumbbell hanging from one side. Now bend very slowly as far to that side as you can. Return slowly to an erect position. See Figures 8-32a and 8-32b.

Figure 8-32a.   **Figure 8-32b.**

TWISTS
External obliques

One of the problems that frequently plagues middle–aged (and sometimes younger) men and women is the development of "love handles" or fatty deposits along the upper hips and waist. Although weight training cannot remove this fat directly, it can tighten the underlying muscle tissue to firm the waist once the fat has been removed by proper diet and continued training. Since the obliques are the muscles that twist and turn the body, it is these, along with the abdominals, that we must focus on. You will need two items, a bench that can be straddled, and a mop, broom handle or bar.

To begin, straddle the bench, back straight, and eyes looking straight ahead. Place the broomstick behind your neck and across your shoulders, placing each hand a few inches from the ends. Squeeze the bench just tightly enough with your knees to prevent your hips from rotating with your shoulders.

Now with your pelvis locked, twist your shoulders and upper trunk as far as they will go to the left. Without stopping, return to the neutral position then twist as far as you can to the right. Start with 25 to 30 repetitions on each side and work up to 100 or more. This exercise may also be done from a standing position, but it is easier to lock your hips if in a sitting position. Figures 8-33a and 8-33b show this exercise.

Figure 8-33a.   **Figure 8-33b.**

LOWER BACK

Forward Bends

Along with lack of flexibility in the hamstring, buttocks, and lower back area, one of the most common causes of lower back pain and injury is weakness of the lower back musculature. The forward lean concentrates on strengthening this area. A few words of caution are appropriate before describing this and the next lift. The literature on back injury indicates that the risk of lower back injury is increased the further a weight is lifted away from the front of the body. Therefore, these lifts should be done slowly and with low resistance, especially if you are just beginning your program. If you have any history of chronic back injury, you should avoid both these lifts until you consult with your physician concerning the reason for the problem and the implications of strengthening the musculature with reference to your condition. Both of these exercises, however,can strengthen the back and add flexibility, since gravity helps to stretch the back when the weight provides a load.

To begin, place a very light weight across your shoulders and bend your knees slightly. Then bend forward at the waist until you begin to feel an easy stretch, and straighten to a standing–tall position prior to the next rep. A backward lean and shoulder shrug as you straighten up will help to loosen your muscles and make you feel more comfortable. See Figure 8-34.

Figure 8-34.

Stiff-Legged Dead Lift
Lower back, hamstring, buttocks, calves

This exercise has also been called the "good morning" exercise. When performing it, be sure to keep the weights as close to the body as is comfortable throughout the lift. And, as with the Forward Bend, move slowly, control the speed, and start light. To perform the lift, place feet shoulder–width apart on a platform. Grasp the bar or dumbbells with the knuckles pointing forward, and slowly bend at the waist to the lowest possible depth. Hang a few seconds and return to the starting position. Remember this will act as both a strengthening exercise and a stretch, and, as with any stretch, ballistic movements are dangerous. This is especially true if they are done with resistance, as is the case with this lift. So don't bounce! Figures 8-35a and 8-35b illustrate the exercise.

Figure 8-35a.   **Figure 8-35b.**

THIGHS AND HIPS

Side Kicks
Hip abductors, buttocks, quadriceps

Side kicks or leg splits with or without added resistance can be very effective in firming the sides of the hips and outer thigh muscles. To perform the exercise, lie on one hip with your upper arm in a position to stabilize your body. Keeping the legs straight, kick up to a comfortable level, then slowly lower the leg to the starting position. In pictures 8-36a and 8-36b, please note how a number 10 food can has been converted into an inexpensive weighted sandal. Most sporting goods store also sell ankle weights or weight shoes that can be used for this purpose.

Figure 8-36a.

Figure 8-36b.

LEGS

Parallel Squat
Quadriceps femoris, gluteus muscles, hamstrings,
and all knee and hip extensors

The squat has been called the "king of exercises" for developing leg strength and power. It is also highly effective for toning and firming inner and outer thigh muscles for women. For years, there has been a controversy concerning the possibility of knee injury during deep squats. Although the results are inconclusive, the possibility of injury has prompted us to describe the parallel squat, so called since it stops when the upper leg is parallel to the ground. A number of important safety precautions should be mentioned since this exercise is a pinned exercise commonly done with very heavy resistance.

First, the breathing on this exercise varies from the usual exhale on the positive, inhale on the negative recommended throughout the text. Since it has been shown that interabdominal pressure protects the back from injury during this lift, the suggested breathing pattern is to inhale as you descend to the parallel position, hold your breath as you begin the ascent and then exhale as the legs begin to straighten (approximately 120° to 130°).

Second, research has shown that stress on the lower back is directly related to forward lean, so the body should be kept as straight as possible, and forward lean should be avoided throughout the lift. In addition, the bar must be well–balanced laterally to reduce the possibility of torquing the back during the lift.

Third, the spotter does not grasp the bar, and he is behind the lifter. These points are important, since the spotter can help the lifter with the weight, as well as maintenance of form, with this high–waist spotting technique. This position also allows for escape for both the lifter and the spotter if necessary. In the past, it was often recommended that a knee–high bench be placed behind the lifter to insure that his or her thighs remained approximately parallel to the floor at the deepest point of the squat. This practice has proven more dangerous than helpful, since the lifters tended to relax on contact with the bench or attempted to use it to push off during the later reps of a fatiguing set. Both practices are potentially dangerous to the lifter's lower back.

There are a number of squat racks and devices, like the Smith machine shown in Chapter 3, that can provide an added measure of safety during the lift. The use of a board or plate under the heels helps if the lifter has trouble keeping his or her heels on the floor during the downward movement. While this may be effective, it shifts the center of gravity forward. In addition, it eliminates the stretch, which is a natural part of the lift and corrects the tightness in the gastrocnemius, soleus, and hamstrings which is responsible for this lack of flexibility. If you must use a heel block, keep reducing it and eliminate it as soon as possible.

When performing the lift, the bar should be held on a squat rack slightly lower than your shoulders. To begin, turn your back to the bar, slide back, bend your knees, and place your shoulders under the bar (see Figure 8-37a). Then gently straighten your legs so that the bar rests on the shoulders and behind the neck. If the bar is too uncomfortable as it presses against the neck vertebrae, you may wish to wrap it in towels or some other soft material.

Now sink downward until your thighs are parallel to the floor, keeping your heels down (see Figure 8-37b). During this downward movement, you should concentrate on keeping the head up and the back as straight up as possible. Two things can help you accomplish this: first, pick a point slightly above your head on the wall in front of you and watch it throughout the lift; and, second, concentrate on keeping the hips from drifting backward to prevent excessive bending at the waist. Once you have reached the parallel position, maintain your posture and rise until your knees are fully straightened.

We suggest that you practice the movement without a weight by extending your hands directly in front of your body, parallel to the floor and attempting the lift while concentrating on that point on the wall and the hip drift. Watch your form in a mirror and/ or have a friend evaluate it. Then, try the lift with a light bar and finally with light weights, before trying the lift at an actual working weight.

If you seriously work at this exercise, it will not be long before you will be able to squat with more weight than you can lift overhead. At this point, you will either require assistance in the form of friends or a pair of adjustable squat racks. As you approach the heavier weights, you may require two spotters, one at either end of the bar.

Figure 8-37a.   Figure 8-37b.

Lunges
Quadriceps, gluteus, hamstrings, groin, hip extensors

To perform this exercise, place a barbell in the same shoulder rest position as describe above for the parallel squat, or you may use two heavy dumbbells with the hands at your sides. Assume an erect posture, and lunge forward by taking a long step and bending the front knee until the thigh is parallel to the floor. Then slowly recover to the standing position. Obviously, this exercise should be done on both sides. You should also realize that the weight is much less than that for the squat. Just as with the squat, you should keep the back straight and control the speed of the movement. This exercise has a strong eccentric component and also provides an excellent stretch for the groin and hamstrings. See Figures 8-38a and 8-38b.

Figure 8-38a.   Figure 8-38b.

LOWER LEG

Toe Raise
Gastrocnemius and soleus

These muscles are often cited as the most difficult to develop; however, there is one excellent exercise which can be used to develop the calf, and that is the toe raise. Actually, this exercise is misnamed, since it is actually the heel of the foot which is raised. However, we will maintain the precedent and use the name toe raise.

This exercise involves placing a barbell across the shoulders or holding dumbbells in your hands, then placing your toes and balls of your feet on a short piece of two–by–four lumber. Now, rise on your toes as high as possible, and then slowly lower yourself to the starting position. See Figures 8-39a and 8-39b. Since the gastrocnemius extends across the knee and ankle, and the soleus only spans the ankle joint, it is believed that bending the legs more will be more specific for the lower part of the calf (soleus), while straightening the legs more will concentrate more work on the gastrocnemius or upper part of the calf.

Figure 8-39a.   **Figure 8-39b.**

Another good exercise which isolates the lower calf is the seated toe raise. You will remember that we showed a toe raise machine in Chapter 3, but it can also be performed with free weights as demonstrated in Figure 8-40. To perform the exercise, place a pad across your thighs for greater comfort. Now, place the barbell across your thighs and again use the board so as to obtain a full stretch.

Figure 8-40.

It is believed that you can target specific areas of the calf by changing foot positions. While we are unaware of any studies which confirm this idea, it has gained such wide acceptance that we present it here for your information. The heels–close and toes–out position is believed to work the inner muscles more, and a heels–out and toes–in position is believed to target the outer calf muscles. Figures 8-41a and 8-41b show each position.

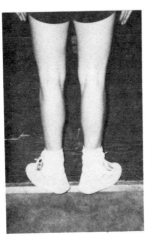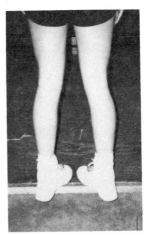

Figure 8-41a.   **Figure 8-41b.**

This chapter represents only a sample of the exercises that have been and will be developed using free weights. As we have stated earlier, one of the advantages of free weights is freedom of movement. This is especially important to those wishing to develop strength and power in sports–specific movements that occur through multiple planes of motion. The samples we have presented provide the reader with a large number of options for targeting all the major muscle groups.

The Universal Machine

LEGS

Universal—regular leg press

1. Lower foot position pedals.
2. Extend legs fully so that knees are straight.
3. Slowly return to flexed position with weight under control.

Universal—calf, ankle, arch press

1. Lower foot position pedals.
2. Extend legs fully pressing with toes and ball of foot.
3. When knees are straight, extend arches and toes as far as possible.
4. Repeat movement.

Figure 9-1a: Leg Press.

Figure 9-1b.

125

Universal—leg extension
Quadriceps

1. Sit upright on table.
2. Place top of foot below the roller.
3. Hold on to the table with both hands and lift both legs together.
4. When fully extended, flex both thighs.
5. Lower weight very slowly to starting position.

Figure 9-2a: Leg extension.   **Figure 9-2b.**

Universal—leg curl
Hamstrings

1. Assume standing position with hands on grips.
2. Place heel under roller with knees pointing straight ahead.
3. Pull heel as far as possible toward buttocks.
4. **Slowly** return to original position.

Figure 9-3.

Universal—toe raises

1. Assume sitting position.
2. Place foot on foot pads and adjust height of knee pads for proper fit.
3. Raise weight by lifting heels.

Figure 9-4a: Toe raises.

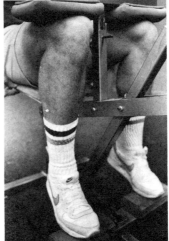

Figure 9-4b.

CHEST, BACK AND ARMS

Universal parallel dip
Pectorals

1. Jump to hang support bending knees slightly and crossing legs at ankles. See Figure 9-5a.
2. Slowly lower body until forearms are at a 45° angle or greater. See Figure 9-5b.
3. Straighten arms assuming original position.
4. Do not move legs up and down. Force the arms to do all of the work.
5. Negative work may be accomplished by doing just the lowering phase, but this must be done very slowly (five seconds).

Figure 9-5a: Parallel dip.   **Figure 9-5b.**

Universal—bench press

1. Lie flat on the bench with your head close to the machine.
2. The bend of handles should be above the chest and your feet should be on the floor.
3. Press weight up while exhaling; return weights slowly and under control.

Figure 9-6a: Bench press.   **Figure 9-6b.**

Universal—upright rowing

1. Adjust chain and bar so that bar rests across thighs at arm's length.
2. Slowly pull bar to chin. See Figure 9-7b.
3. Slowly allow arms to move back to original position.

Note: It should take approximately twice the time to lower a weight as it does to raise it.

Figure 9-7a: Upright rowing.   **Figure 9-7b.**

Universal—seated press

1. Sit facing machine, shoulders almost touching handles. See Figure 9-8a.
2. If possible, place feet inside rungs of bench. This will prevent pushing with your legs.
3. Press upward, trying to keep back flat, and exhaling as the arms move up. Think about blowing the weight up. See Figure 9-8b.

Figure 9-8a: Universal seated press.   **Figure 9-8b.**

Universal—behind neck press

1. Assume a seated position facing the bar.
2. Arms should be fully extended with a wide grip on the bar. See Figure 9-9a.
3. Tilt head forward and pull bar to base of neck. Exhale as the bar comes down, inhale as it goes up. See Figure 9-9b.

Figure 9-9a: Behind neck press.   **Figure 9-9b.**

Universal—chinning

1. Assume a shoulder–width grip.
2. Fully extend then pull to chin level.

Note: Moving hands closer together and farther apart will work your arms more completely. Shifting grips to both overhand and underhand also helps. If you have a tendency to swing, touch floor lightly with toes after each descent.

Figure 9-10: Chinning.

Universal—triceps extension

1. Assume erect standing position—palms down, hands fairly close together, and elbows in. See Figure 9-11a.
2. Bring bar to shoulder height. Press down and extend arms. Exhale down, inhale up. See Figure 9-11b.

Note: Reduce weight if cable touches body.

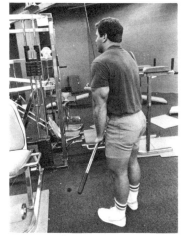

Figure 9-11a: Triceps extension.　**Figure 9-11b.**

Universal—shoulder shrug

There are three ways to do the shoulder shrug:

1. Lift straight up and down.
2. Rotate shoulders in a forward circle.
3. Rotate shoulders in a backward circle.

Figure 9-12a: Shoulder shrug.　**Figure 9-12b.**

Universal—curls (regular and reverse)

1. Assume palms–up grip—arms extended.
2. Raise bar to near chin level.
3. Slowly lower bar to original position.
4. Repeat process.

Note: To perform the reverse curl, turn palms toward floor.

Figure 9-13a: Arm curl.

Figure 9-13b.

Universal—wrist roller

1. **Regular wrist curl:** Place hands on grips, palms down. Bend wrists *away* from you.
2. **Reverse wrist curl:** Bend wrists *toward* you.
3. **Pronated wrist curl:** Place hands on the door knob end and rotate in both directions.

Figure 9-13b.

10

The Nautilus System

In this chapter, you will be guided through the use of the equipment that started the hi–tech revolution in resistance training, the Nautilus machines. In 1970, Arthur Jones introduced the concept of varying resistance by using a spiral cam to adjust the leverage offered by his machine to the mechanical advantages and disadvantages of the body.

As he studied the shape of the cams he had designed, it occurred to him that they resembled the chambered nautilus shell, and that was the name he gave to his now–famous line of exercise equipment.

Arthur Jones' concept of matching the biomechanical strengths and leverage is brilliant in its simplicity. The Nautilus machines combine the benefits of joint isolation and muscle–specific movement with the accommodating resistance concept, to produce a line of exercise equipment designed for an efficient, full–body workout with minimal risk of injury. Since these machines control the movements and define the range of motion, you can begin training after reviewing a few of the basic concepts already discussed in previous chapters. These concepts include:

1. Controlling the speed of movement throughout the exercise with emphasis on slower movement through the eccentric contraction. We usually recommend a two- to three-second count on the concentric and twice as long for the eccentric phase. Note: Due to the pulley and chain nature of these cam machines, they are not well suited for power training.

2. Perform all lifts through the full range of motion. The Nautilus group is designed to stretch the muscles and connective tissues at the ends of the ranges of motion. Push all concentric movements until the mechanical stops on the machine are reached. When performing the eccentric phase, allow the weights to **gently** touch the stack.

3. Line up the joint being exercised with the shaft or pivot point of the machine. This will put you in the correct position to execute the lift. Once you are in line, maintain that position and do the lift using strict form. Millions of dollars were spent to design these machines so that the specific muscles to be exercised could be isolated. You waste money, time and training by "dancing" around on the machine. Some women complain that some of the machines are too large and that it is difficult to align themselves correctly. Most gyms will have accessory pads which allow a smaller person to make good use of the equipment. Ask for these pads and use them.

4. Work the larger muscle groups first. This will allow you to do the gross movements requiring greater weight at the beginning of the workout.

5. Allow a 48-hour recovery period between workouts.

6. Always wear proper shoes when using the machines. (Some of the photos in this chapter show ballet slippers and bare feet in the weight room. This is extremely dangerous.)

One last note on repetitions and sets: It has been stated that these machines require only one set of 8–12 repetitions to exhaustion for an optimal workout. At this point, you should be aware that the number of repetitions you decide to use is dependent on the results you desire. Literature has confirmed that at least three sets are necessary for maximal benefit. This is not to say that you will not improve using the one set, 8–12 rep system, only that you will not progress as quickly as with a multiple set workout.

DUOsymmetric/POLYcontractile
HIP AND BACK MACHINE

Gluteus maximus, hamstrings, and erector spinae group

1. Enter machine from front by separating movement arms.
2. Lie on back with both legs over roller pads.
3. Align hip joint with axes of cams.
4. Fasten seat belt and grasp handles lightly. Seat belt should be snug, but not too tight, as back must be arched at completion of movement.
5. Extend both legs and at the same time push back with arms.
6. Keep one leg at full extension, allow other leg to bend and come back as far as possible.
7. Stretch.
8. Push out until it joins other leg at extension.
9. Pause, arch lower back, and contract buttocks. In contracted position, keep legs straight, knees together, and toes pointed.
10. Repeat with other leg.

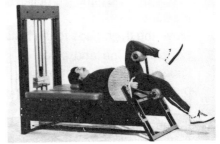

Figure 10-1: Hip and back machine—stretched position, left buttocks; contracted position, right buttocks.

HIP ABDUCTION–ADDUCTION
MACHINE

Hip Abduction
Gluteus medius of outer hip

1. Adjust lever on right side of machine until both movement arms are together.
2. Move thigh pads to the outer position
3. Sit in machine and place knees and ankles on movement arms. The outer thighs and knees should be firmly against the resistance pads.

4. Fasten seat belt.
5. Keep head and shoulders against seat back.
6. Spread knees and thighs to widest possible position.
7. Pause.
8. Return to knees–together position and repeat.

Hip Adduction
Adductor muscles of inner thighs

1. Adjust lever on right side of machine for range of movement. The farther the handle is pulled up, the greater the range of the machine.
2. Move the thigh pads to the inside position.
3. Sit in machine and place knees and ankles on movement arms in a spread-legged position. The inner thighs and knees should be firmly against the resistance pads.

4. Fasten seat belt.
5. Keep head and shoulders against back seat.
6. Pull knees and thighs smoothly together.

Figure 10-2: Hip abduction/adduction machine.

7. Pause in knees–together position.
8. Return slowly to stretched position and repeat.

Important: To better isolate the adductor muscles, keep the feet pointed inward and pull with the thighs, not the lower legs.

MULTI–EXERCISE MACHINE

Calf Raise
1. Adjust belt comfortably around hips.
2. Place balls of feet on first step and hands on front on carriage.
3. Lock knees and keep locked throughout the movement.
4. Elevate heels as high as possible and try to stand on big toes.
5. Pause.

6. Lower heels slowly.
7. Stretch at bottom by lifting toes.
8. Repeat.

Figure 10-3: Multi-exercise machine side bend.   **Figure 10-4:** Multi-exercise machine—toe rise with bend.

Triceps Extension

1. Loop a lightweight towel through weight belt.
2. Grasp ends of towel in each hand. Stand and face away.
3. Adjust grip on towel until weight stack is separated.
4. Straighten arms in a very smooth fashion.
5. Pause.
6. Lower resistance slowly and repeat.

Parallel Dip
(negative only, with or without weight belt)

1. Adjust carriage to proper level. It is important to stretch in bottom position.
2. Climb steps.
3. Lock elbows and bend legs.
4. Lower body slowly by bending arms (8–10 seconds).
5. Stretch at bottom position.
6. Climb up and repeat.

Chin–up
(negative only, with or without weight belt)

1. Place cross–bar on forward position.
2. Adjust carriage to proper height. When standing on top step, chin should be barely over bar.
3. Grasp cross–bar with palms up.
4. Climb steps.
5. Place chin over bar, elbows by sides, and legs bent.
6. Lower body slowly (8–10 seconds).
7. Stretch at bottom position.
8. Climb up and repeat.

Important: Movement can also be done in a behind neck fashion by using parallel grip.

Wrist curl

1. Sit in front of machine, using small bench or chair, with toes under first step.
2. Attach small bar directly to movement arm.
3. Grasp handles in a palms–up fashion. (Palms–down grip should also be used.)
4. Place forearms firmly against thighs.
5. Curl small bar upward.
6. Pause.
7. Lower resistance slowly and repeat.

Important: Do not move forearms. Only hands should move. Keep knees close together. Avoid jerky movements. Other movements include: Biceps curl, Shoulder shrug, Bent–over row, Hanging leg raise and Side bend.

Abdominal Machine
Rectus abdominis

1. Sit in machine.
2. Locate axis of rotation on right side.
3. Adjust seat so axis of rotation is at same level as lower part of sternum or breastbone.

4. Place ankles behind roller pads.
5. Spread knees and sit erect.
6. Grasp handles.
7. Keep shoulders and head firmly against seat back.
8. Shorten the distance between rib cage and navel by contracting abdominals only. Do not pull with latissimus or triceps muscles.
9. Keep legs relaxed as seat bottom is elevated.
10. Pause in contracted position.
11. Return slowly to starting position and repeat.

Figure 10-5: Abdominal machine.

COMPOUND LEG MACHINE

Leg Extension
Frontal thighs or quadriceps

1. Place feet behind roller pads, with knees snug against seat.
2. Adjust seat back to comfortable position.
3. Keep head and shoulders against seat back.
4. Straighten both legs smoothly.
5. Pause.
6. Lower resistance slowly and repeat.
7. Move quickly to leg press after final repetition.

Leg Press
Quadriceps, hamstrings, and gluteus maximus

1. Sit erect and pull seat back forward.
2. Flip down foot pads.
3. Place both feet on pads with toes pointed slightly inward.

4.   Straighten both legs in a controlled manner.

5.   Return to stretched position and repeat.

Important: Avoid tightly gripping handles and do not grit teeth or tense neck or face muscles during either movement.

Figure 10-6a: Compound leg machine—leg extension, beginning position.

Figure 10-6b: Compound leg machine—leg extension, finished position.

Figure 10-7: Compound leg machine—leg press, finished position.

Leg Curl Machine
Hamstrings

1. Lie face down on machine.
2. Place feet under roller pads with knees just over edge of bench.
3. Grasp handles to keep body moving.
4. Curl legs and try to touch heels to buttocks.
5. Lift buttocks to increase range of motion.
6. Pause at point of full contraction.
7. Lower resistance slowly and repeat.

Important: Top of foot should be flexed toward knee throughout movement.

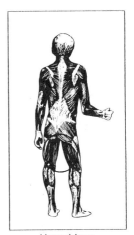

Figure 10-8: Leg curl machine—full hamstring contraction.

Hamstrings

DOUBLE CHEST MACHINE

Arm Cross
Pectoralis majors of the chest and deltoids of shoulders

1. Adjust seat until shoulders, when elbows are together, are directly under axes of overhead cams.
2. Fasten seat belt.
3. Place handles lightly and firmly against movement arm pads.

4. Grasp handles lightly, thumbs should be around handle, and keep head against seat back.
5. Push with forearms and try to touch elbows together in front of chest. (Movement can also be done one arm at a time in an alternate fashion.)
6. Pause.
7. Lower resistance slowly and repeat. After final repetition, immediately do decline press.

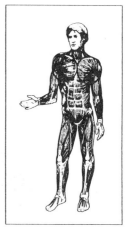

Figure 10-9: Double chest machine—arm cross, beginning position.

Figure 10-10: Double chest machine—decline press.

Pectoralis majors of the chest and deltoids of the shoulders.

Decline press
Chest, shoulders, and triceps of arms

1. Use foot pedal to raise handles into starting position.
2. Grasp handles with parallel grip.
3. Keep head back and torso erect.
4. Press bars forward in controlled fashion.
5. Lower resistance slowly keeping elbows wide.
6. Stretch in bottom position and repeat pressing movement.

DOUBLE SHOULDER MACHINE

Lateral Raise
Deltoid muscles of shoulders

1. Adjust seat so shoulder joints are in line with axes of cams.
2. Position thighs on seat, cross ankles, and fasten seat belt.
3. Pull handles back until knuckles touch pads.
4. Lead with elbows and raise both arms until parallel with floor.
5. Pause.
6. Lower resistance slowly and repeat. After final repetition, immediately do overhead press.

Important: Keep knuckles against pads and elbows high at all times.

Figure 10-11: Double shoulder machine—lateral raise contracted position.

Overhead Press
Deltoids and triceps

1. Raise seat quickly for greater range of movement.
2. Grasp handles above shoulders.
3. Press handles overhead while being careful not to arch back.
4. Lower resistance slowly keeping elbows wide, and repeat.

Pullover Machine (Plateloading)
Latissimus dorsi of the back and other torso muscles

1. Adjust seat so shoulder joints are in line with axes of cams.
2. Assume erect position and fasten seat belt tightly.
3. Leg press foot pedal until elbows pads are about chin level.
4. Place elbows on pads. Hands should be open and resting on curved portion of bar.

5. Remove legs from pedal and slowly rotate elbows as far back as possible.
6. Stretch.
7. Rotate elbows down until bar touches midsection.
8. Pause.
9. Return slowly to stretch position and repeat.

Important: Look straight ahead during movement. Do not move head or torso. Do not grip tightly with hands.

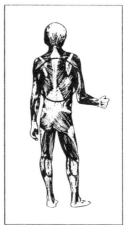

Figure 10-12: Pullover machine, stretched position.

Latissimus dorsi muslces of the back and other torso muscles, including abdominals.

COMBINATION BEHIND NECK AND TORSO ARM MACHINE

Behind neck

Latissimus dorsi of the back

1. Adjust seat so shoulder joints are in line with axes of cams.
2. Fasten seat belt.
3. Place back of upper arms (triceps area) between padded movement arms.
4. Cross forearms behind neck.

5. Move both arms down until perpendicular to floor.
6. Pause.
7. Return slowly to crossed–arm position behind neck.

Important: Be careful not to bring arms or hands to front of body.

Behind Neck Pulldown
Latissimus dorsi of the back and biceps of upper arm

1. Lean forward and grasp overhead bar with parallel grip.
2. Pull bar behind neck, keeping elbows back.
3. Pause.
4. Return slowly to start position and repeat.

Figure 10-13a: Behind neck and torso arm machine—pulldown.

Figure 10-13b: Behind neck machine, finished position.

Rowing Machine
Deltoids and trapezius

1. Sit with back toward weight stack.
2. Place arms between pads and cross arms.
3. Bend arms in rowing fashion as far back as possible.
4. Pause.
5. Return slowly to starting position and repeat.

Important: Keep arms parallel to floor at all times.

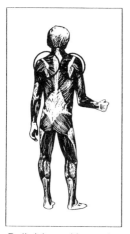

Deltoids and trapezius   Trapezius and back
of neck

Figure 10-14: Rowing machine,
extended position.

Neck and Shoulder
Trapezius and back of neck

1. Place forearms between pads while seated.
2. Keep palms open and back of hands pressed against bottom
    pads.
3. Straighten torso until weight
    stack is lifted. Seat may be
    raised with elevation pads.
4. Shrug shoulders smoothly as
    high as possible.
5. Pause.
6. Return slowly to stretching
    position and repeat.

Important: Keep elbows by sides
when shrugging. Do not lean back
or try to stand while doing the
movement. Do not rest weights
on stack during movement.

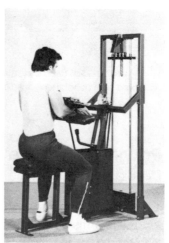

Figure 10-15: Neck and shoulder
machine—shoulder shrug.

Compound Position Curl Machine
Biceps of the upper arm

1. Be seated on the left side of the machine to work the right biceps.
2. Adjust the seat so the elbow is in line with the axis of the cam.
3. Grasp the handle lightly with an underhand grip.
4. Curl the handle behind the heck.
5. Pause.
6. Lower the movement arm slowly and repeat.
7. Reverse the procedure for working the left biceps on the right side of the machine.

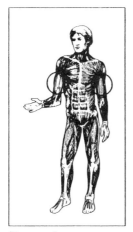

Biceps of upper arms

Figure 10-16: Compound curl machine, beginning position.

Multi–Biceps Machine
Biceps of upper arms

1. Place elbows on pad and in line with the axes of cams.
2. Adjust seat so shoulders are slightly lower than elbows. Machine can be used in at least eight different ways.

Two arm normal

1. Curl both arms to the contracted position.
2. Pause.
3. Lower slowly to the stretched position and repeat.

Two arms alternate

1. Do a complete repetition with one arm.
2. Do another complete repetition with the opposite arm.
3. Alternate until momentary muscular exhaustion.

Figure 10-17: Multi-biceps machine.

Two arms duo–poly

1. Bring both arms to the contracted position.
2. Holding one arm in the contracted position, lower the resistance with the opposite arm, and curl the movement arm back to the contracted position.
3. Repeat with other arm.

Important: One arm must always be in the contracted position while the other arm is moving.

One arm normal

1. Work the non–dominant arm to exhaustion first.
2. Work the other arm to exhaustion.

Note: A trainee will be able to handle slightly more resistance with one arm than with two.

One arm negative emphasized

1. Use the opposite arm for assistance in curling heavier–than–normal weight.
2. Lower slowly the resistance arm (8–10 seconds) with one arm.
3. Continue in this fashion until the biceps is unable to control the downward movement.
4. Repeat the procedure with the other arm.

With The Movement Restraining Stop
In The Center Position:

Infimetric

Remove the selector pin from the weight stack. Curl both arms to the mid–range position, or until contact is made with the movement restraining stop. In order for one arm to straighten, the other arm must bend. The trainee can vary the force by resisting more or less with the unbending arm. The movement should be smooth and steady with no dropping of the weight.

Isometric

Same procedure as infimetric, except do not permit movement of the unbending arm. Since a person is 40 percent stronger negatively than positively, the negative arm is always able to prevent movement in the positive arm. It is possible, therefore, to provide an isometric or static contraction at any point along the range of movement of the machine.

Akinetic

The primary difference between infimetric and akinetic is in infimetric the selector pin is not used, while in akinetic predetermined amount of resistance is used. With infimetric training, it is very difficult to estimate the amount of force that is being exerted during the movement. With akinetic training, however, a medium resistance is selected and although trainees can exert more force, any time they exert less force, the weight stack drops noticeably.

Multi–Triceps Machine
Triceps of upper arms

1. Adjust seat so shoulders are slightly lower than elbow.
2. Place sides of hands on movement arms and elbows on pad and in line with the axes of cams. Machine can be used in at least eight different ways.

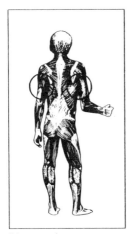

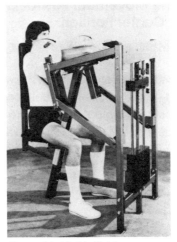

Triceps of upper arms   **Figure 10-18:** Multi–triceps machine.

Two arms normal

1. Straighten arms to the contracted position.
2. Pause.
3. Lower slowly to the stretched position and repeat.

Lower arm duo–poly

1. Straighten both arms to the contracted position.
2. Holding one arm in the contracted position, lower the resistance with the opposite arm, and return to the contracted position.
3. Repeat with the other arm.

One arm normal

1. Work one arm to exhaustion, usually the non–dominant arm first.
2. Work the other arm to exhaustion.

Note: A trainee will be able to handle slightly more resistance with one arm than two.

Two arm negative–emphasized

1. Use the opposite arm for assistance in lifting a heavier–than–normal weight.
2. Lower slowly the resistance arm (8–10 seconds) with one arm.
3. Continue in this fashion until the triceps is unable to control the downward movement.
4. Repeat the procedure with the other arm.

BICEPS/TRICEPS MACHINE (Plateloading)

Biceps Curl
Biceps of upper arm

1. Enter machine from left side.
2. Place elbows on pad and in line with axis of cam.
3. Grasp bar with hands together and palms up.
4. Curl bar smoothly until it reaches neck.
5. Pause.
6. Return slowly to stretched position and repeat.
Important: Lean back at full extension to ensure stretching.

Triceps Extension
Triceps of upper arms

1. Adjust seated position, with pads if necessary, until shoulders are on same level as elbows.
2. Place elbows in line with axis of cam and hands with thumbs up on pads.
3. Straighten arms smoothly.
4. Pause.
5. Return slowly to stretched position and repeat.

Figure 10-19: Biceps/triceps machine.

ALL-PURPOSE MACHINE

Triceps Extension

1. Loop a lightweight towel through weight belt.
2. Grasp one end of towel in each hand. Stand and face away from machine.
3. Arms should now be bent with elbows by ears.
4. Adjust grip on towel until weight stack is separated.
5. Straighten arms in a very smooth fashion.
6. Pause.
7. Slowly lower resistance and repeat.

Figure 10-20a: All-purpose machine—triceps extension, beginning position.

Figure 10-20b: All-purpose machine—triceps extension, ending position.

FOUR-WAY NECK MACHINE

Anterior Flexion

Front of neck

1. Face machine.
2. Adjust seat so nose is in center of pads.
3. Stabilize torso by lightly grasping handles.
4. Move head smoothly toward chest.

5. Pause.
6. Return slowly to stretching position and repeat.
Important: Do not use torso or legs to assist neck. Good form is a must.

Rotation of neck and head to right and left.   **Figure 10-21:** Four-way neck machine.

Posterior Extension
Back of neck

1. Turn body machine until back of head contacts center of pads.
2. Stabilize torso by lightly grasping handles.
3. Extend head as far back as possible.
4. Pause.
5. Return slowly to stretched position and repeat.

Lateral Contraction
Side of neck

1. Turn body in machine until left ear is in center of pads.
2. Stabilize torso by lightly grasping handles.
3. Move head toward left shoulder.
4. Pause.
5. Keep shoulders square.
6. Return slowly to stretched position and repeat.
7. Reverse procedure for right side.

One final note on Nautilus training: Many of the machines in the line were produced without weights given for the plates. This may have been an excellent idea, since it allowed the user to concentrate on performance of the correct form as opposed to the amount of weight lifted. However, humans are a competitive species and will compete to see who gets the higher letter or number, so this psychology doesn't usually work. In addition, most people are goal–oriented, and like to know how much they are lifting. Therefore, we can offer you this generalization: The top plate on all Nautilus machines with self–contained weight stacks weighs 10 pounds. The selector rod weighs 10 pounds also. Thus, the lightest weight available is 20 pounds. Each plate weighs 10 pounds. To put 50 pounds on the pullover machine, the individual counts the top plate and selector rod as 20 and places the selector pin in the third hole from the top. Remember, however, that 10 pounds on a machine that varies your mechanical advantage throughout the range of motion will not feel the same as 10 pounds of free weight. Also if smaller increments in weight are required, many gyms have light weights (2.5 or 5 pounds) which can be slipped over the weight stacks.

11

Questions Most Often Asked

Is physical fitness important to good health?
The resounding answer to this question is yes.
There is little doubt that exercise is medicine, and
that, all things being equal, the physically fit person can expect to enjoy a healthier, longer life.
The only thing that complicates this question is
the term *physical fitness.* Since this term encom-
passes a number of different measures such as
muscular strength, muscular endurance, cardiovascular condition, flexibility, and body composition, it would probably be better to examine each
of these separately when answering this question.
In addition, you should realize that there is not a
linear relationship between fitness and health.
When we see the elite athlete, who may run 40 or
more miles a week, he or she is not necessarily
twice as healthy as the runner who does 20 miles
a week. The person who can bench press 400
pounds is not four times as healthy as the individual who can only lift 100 pounds. Fitness is
made up of a number of separate components,
and exercise should be prescribed according to
the needs and goals of the individual.

Will I be physically fit if I weight train? This question relates directly to the first. And if we look at one specific component of physical fitness, strength, the answer is obviously yes. If you are asking about cardiovascular (heart, blood vessels, and lungs) fitness, then the answer varies according to the program you choose. As you remember from Chapters 4 and 5, you can change the lifting method and better target cardiovascular improvement if that is your goal. However, the level of strength gained will not be as great.

What are the latest statistics on low back pain and its causes? Low back pain is a major health problem. With about 70 million chronic cases and nearly seven million new cases yearly, many people are becoming dependent upon medication for pain. Injuries and a number of other disorders continue to trigger this condition. Researchers have determined, however, that most low back pain problems result from muscle tension, muscle weakness and muscle spasms, a strong argument for selected weight training exercises. There has been a great interest in the diagnosis of specific areas of weakness in the lower back musculature and prescriptive exercise to reduce its impact on the individual. A number of companies, such as Medex, have concentrated on the diagnosis and selective strengthening of the lower back musculature.

Can weight training prevent osteoporosis (loss of bone)? While this question cannot be answered absolutely, all the scientific evidence to date has been positive. The two groups most affected by this are post–menopausal females and elderly males, since both groups experience natural reductions in bone mass. Data from laboratory animals has shown positive effects of weight training on bone mass. Significant losses in bone mass have been reported in astronauts after prolonged exposure to the low–gravity environment of space. Since bone is a living tissue capable of change in reaction to the stresses placed upon it, there is every reason to believe that resistance training will increase the bone mass of aging males and females. It also appears that the increases in bone mass are specific to the bones used. Therefore, the use of such exercises as the squat, overhead press or other movements that put compressive forces on the spinal column offer

offer the highest potential for reducing the bone loss in the vertebrae associated with aging. Of course, proper blood calcium levels are necessary. In some cases, estrogen and vitamin supplementation for women who have reached menopause are also necessary.

Can weight training cause a rupture? Hard coughing can cause a rupture. Anyone who is predisposed to ruptures can sustain one by straining. One researcher who collected information on weight training injuries found the evidence of hernia to be 20 times less among weight trainers than among an average group of people.

YES

What about smoking and weight training? There is at present overwhelming evidence to indicate that smoking is one of the most dangerous habits engaged in by men and women. Smoking only one pack a day increases a person's risk of a heart attack three times over that of a nonsmoker.

DON'T

Smoking also seriously diminishes your maximum exercise capacity. McHenry, at the Indiana University School for Medicine reported that when a group of state policemen were divided into three groups and exercised to maximum capacity, the nonsmokers were able to exercise the longest. In this experiment, subjects were classified into three groups: smokers, former smokers who had quit at least one year, and nonsmokers. Other findings were as follows:

1. Nonsmokers had lower systolic blood pressure levels than smokers, an indication of superior blood vessel health.
2. Smokers developed faster heart rates at the same levels of exercise than did nonsmokers. This indicates the inefficiency of the entire cardiovascular system, since the heart worked harder to do the same level of work.
3. Former smokers had approximately the same blood pressure levels as nonsmokers, although those with previous history of very heavy smoking were not able to exercise as long as the nonsmokers.

It is a sad commentary that every year we continue to lose almost as many Americans to smoking as were killed in all of World War II. However, the national percentage of smokers continues to drop. Doctors who smoke have steadily decreased to about 21 percent. It is a slow process, but we are making some progress.

WEIGHT TRAINING AND AGE

Is there a point in life when it is too late to begin an exercise program? The good news is that it is never too late to begin. The latest research on weight training and the elderly has shown that persons in their nineties can still significantly increase their muscle mass and strength. The section on aging and the older individual in Chapter 12 covers this in greater detail.

What is the best age for young people to begin strength training? Most doctors advise ages 14 to 16. However, as we know, our athletic programs begin earlier than that. Many coaches and trainers believe that strength training should begin around ages eight to ten, but in the form of games, rather than formal weight training. There had been some concern about potential damage to the growth plates in the bones of these younger lifters. In nearly all reported cases, however, the injury occurred during unsupervised lifting. Games such as football, basketball or baseball have demonstrated a much higher potential for this type of injury than weight training. But it is extremely important to realize that weight training uses large external stresses to increase muscle size, and younger participants should be carefully monitored to reduce the possibility of injury from incorrect technique or horseplay.

Is it true there has been a drop in the number of exercisers in the last few years? A recent Gallup Poll says yes. Dr. Kenneth Cooper believes that if the trend toward inactivity and obesity among young people continues, the whole wellness program is in jeopardy.

Other reliable sources report the same thing. In 1982, The Institute for Aerobics Research began a youth fitness program called FITNESSGRAM. Today, the original plan has evolved into a nationwide program involving more than three million students and sponsored by the Campbell Soup Company. Where earliest tests place heavy emphasis on athletic skills, the FITNESSGRAM places heavy emphasis on health–related measurements of true body fitness.

In the 1986-87 school year, more than 170,000 students were compared with a group tested in 1975. The results ranged from no improvement to declines in every event. The greatest losses were in the areas of body composition and cardiovascular endurance.

Another study conducted by the Public Health Service in 1985, the National Children and Youth Fitness Study, found that young people have more body fat and weigh more than they did 20 years ago. The study also found that at least one–third are not experiencing aerobic benefits due to a lack of physical activity.

Another study by the same group found a direct relationship between inactivity and fatness among those children having inactive parents and the number of hours children were allowed to view television. In a society where computers and video games have such an impact on our youth, the possibility that children will substitute the imagined activity of a video game for the reality of active play is a constant problem.

decline since 1960

WEIGHT TRAINING AND BODY COMPOSITION

Can I lose weight by weight training? Research indicates that men and women react about the same to a high–resistance weight program. The lean body weight increases and the total body fat decreases. This very often does not do much to change the total body weight and people who are "scale conscious" are often discouraged, even though they are making significant progress. Remember, weight is not the problem. Whether that weight is muscle or bone or fat should be your only concern.

Most researchers agree that the most effective way to lose weight is by a combination of activity and proper dietary habits. Most also agree that a running or aerobic activity is necessary for best results.

How can I tell if I am losing body fat? In addition to weighing yourself regularly, there are a number of other ways to determine if you are making progress in shedding body fat. The best way is to arrange for an assessment of body fat. If you remember the discussion in Chapter 7, underwater weighing is the most accurate method of assessing body fat. Many fitness institutes, exercise physiology labs, and human performance labs offer this service. Other methods include skin pinches, infrared scanning, and electrical impedance measurements. One very simple way is to "pinch" the fat at your waist and see if the fold is getting thicker or thinner. We also recommend standing in front of the mirror and giving yourself an honest assessment.

Although most fat is stored under the skin with the thicker layers around the waist, when you reduce your bodily percentage of fat, it is reduced proportionately from all over the body. Therefore, you can take measurements with a cloth or metal tape and compare the circumferences of various body parts. Remember that not all measurements will decrease. If you lift weights, your arms, legs, and chest will increase or remain the same size. However, if you compare these to your waist and hip measurements, you should see a significant change if you are making progress. It has often been a regular practice of body builders to make such circumferential measurements.

Darden suggests the following rules for recording weekly measurements:

1. Take the measurements before a training session.
2. Use the same cloth tape measure for every measurement.
3. Relax the arm and take the measurement midway between the elbow and tip of the shoulder with the arm hanging away from the body. Record to the nearest 1/16 of an inch.

I have heard and read so much about "proper body fat" that I don't know what to believe. It is true that while most researchers agree upon a fairly narrow range, there is little agreement on an exact percentage. We recommend between 12 and 15 percent for college–aged males and between 18 and 24 percent for college–aged females. These percentages may increase slightly with age due to the greater fat deposits which surround the internal organs as we get older.

Can I gain weight through a progressive program of weight training? The traditional formula for adding weight is to use high resistance and low repetition. In the early 1930's, M. H. Berry promoted the idea of using dead lifts, supine presses, two–arm pullovers, and bent arm pull–overs to gain weight.

Most weight training experts agree that a few heavy exercises will promote weight gain, but not necessarily an attractive body build. They believe the best method of attaining the greatest development and physique is to add the bulk and weight and then to train down to desirable proportions. While this has been a normal practice, it may lead to the unhealthy habit of yo–yo dieting. We suggest that diet become a part of your lifestyle, rather than an abrupt change in lifestyle. Watch your caloric balance while working out, and you will avoid both the discomfort and poor eating habits associated with a yo–yo diet routine.

I am an athlete and am not sure whether I am too fat or too lean. How can I tell? Most experts believe that an athlete who is lean and muscular should have a difference of one to two inches in flexed and unflexed biceps girth. If you have an excess amount of fat on your body, you will have less than a one–inch difference. The leaner you are, the greater the difference.

If I develop muscles and then stop lifting, will they turn to fat? Fat accumulates on almost everyone who eats a lot and exercises little. Well–developed muscle tend to lose size through lack of exercise, so the percentage of body fat and body muscle will likely change, but muscle does not turn to fat—the fat just accumulates.

What about steam and heat? Steam and heat may feel wonderful, and the perspiration may clean the dirt out of your pores. However, the practice of exercising in a high–temperature environment is counterproductive. The fat you lose is dependent on the amount of energy you expend, which is equal to the amount of work you do. The heat of a steam room or sauna causes your core body temperature to rise to a level where the amount of work you can do is limited, so the only weight you will lose is water. This will lead to dehydration, the need to drink, and the regaining of that same water weight.

Will those "body wraps" which I see on television help me to lose weight? The idea that wrapping your body in rags soaked in mud, even if that mud is supposed to be "porous volcanic rock from the center of the earth," is absolutely ridiculous. At best you'll get a nice skin cleansing and need to drink a few glasses of water to replace all the fluid you lose. Any loss of inches is due solely to the water loss and compression of tissue. Both will return to normal soon after the wrap is removed.

How about special belts that inflate, or rubberized air–tight clothing? There is no evidence to substantiate that the wearing of such clothing causes a weight loss or spot reductions of adipose tissue. Such clothing may promote sweating, and therefore, temporary loss of fluids, but it is the exercise that is beneficial. *Avoid rubberized suits.* This type of clothing can be dangerous in hot, humid weather. This attire does not aid in weight reduction, only in temporary water loss. The best clothing is that which is loose, comfortable, absorbent and reflects the sun in hot climates.

Can I reduce the fat on my abdomen or thighs by doing sit-ups or squats? The bad news is that all the research to date indicates that spot reduction is not possible, so you can't selectively target those problem areas. The good news is that if you target these areas, the muscle tissue will become better toned and you will look better at whatever percentage of body fat you're at.

What's a quick fix for poor leg definition? There's no quick fix for anything that has to do with body composition. The best you can do is to use the principles that we have explained on bulk and definition and hope that genetics cooperate.

Can weight training get rid of cellulite? What we commonly call cellulite is nothing more than fat with indentations or stippling. If you want to get rid of cellulite, get rid of body fat. Contrary to the advertisements you may have seen, it can't be scrubbed, burned or massaged away, nor can it be removed by pills.

WEIGHT TRAINING, ANATOMY AND KINESIOLOGY

How many muscles are there in my body? Your body has approximately 600 muscles containing more than six billion microscopic muscle fibers. Even more astounding is that each fiber is so strong that it is able to support more than one thousand times its own weight. The contraction of a well–developed muscle can break the bone to which it is attached.

How can I identify which muscle groups are involved in a given exercise? The easiest way is to read all the information included in this book. However, for any exercise that is not included, remember that the muscles which cause movement at a joint are usually located just above the joint and toward the center of the body. For example, when the lower leg is flexed or extended at the knee joint, the muscles involved are located between the knee joint and the hip joint.

If you have someone provide resistance to your movement, you will be able to feel the surface muscles where the movement is taking place. Those muscles that are firm and hard are the contracting muscles and those that are soft and flexible are the non-contracting or nonworking muscles.

Is working my abdominals with weights going to make my stomach bulge out? I want it flat! Let's settle one thing first, your stomach is an internal organ and won't be affected by weight training one way or the other. As to bulging abdominals, it would seem reasonable that, since muscles hypertrophy with weight training, your abdominals should get larger and "bulge out." However, the abdominals are a very flat, sheetlike muscle, and even the hypertrophy will produce little more than those great looking "cuts" we all like so much! Plus, well–developed abdominals support our internal organs better.

What about body measurements? Carl Sandburg once said, "People lie because they can't help making a story better," and so it is when body builders begin to talk about their body measurements. First, you cannot measure yourself with any degree of accuracy, since you cannot keep the tape from slanting. Second, measurements must be taken before, and not after exercise, because a vigorous workout will temporarily swell your muscles. The tape should be of cloth or steel and you should use the same tape for successive measurements.

What particular kinds of body builds seem to enable physique builders and heavy weight lifters to do best? Most of the Olympic weight lifters tend to have a reasonably long trunk, big bones, thick waist, heavily muscled buttocks, and short arms and legs. Male body builders, on the other hand, tend to have smaller joints, bones, buttocks, waist and hips. This is combined with exceptionally broad shoulders and an excessively large chest.

WEIGHT TRAINING AND DETRAINING

After exercise, how long must I wait to regain my strength? Laboratory experiments indicate that if a muscle is fully fatigued, it will take approximately 45 minutes for full recovery. Under ideal conditions, a muscle will regain 70 percent of its initial strength within 30 seconds and will be able to perform with 80–90 percent of normal strength within seven and a half minutes.

Why should I do my weight program three or four times a week rather than every day? Research indicates little difference in strength gains between a three– or four–day program as opposed to a seven–day program. Also, the body requires a certain amount of rest for repair and growth.

Once I acquire the strength I need, what do I have to do to keep it? Strength can be maintained by exercising at least once weekly. However, all body parts must be exercised at close to maximum repetition. It should be noted that this type of workout may cause muscle soreness.

If I stop exercising, what happens to my gains? Most research indicates that body conditioning acquired after a four–week training program is lost within two weeks if training is discontinued completely.

Is cooling down important? Dr. Kenneth Cooper, noted aerobics expert, suggests the following:
1. **Do** taper off gradually. Walk or jog slowly, since this keeps the blood moving and improves circulation.
2. **Do not** go into a steam room or sauna immediately after working out. Wait until you have stopped sweating.

When will I see results from all this lifting? You should begin to feel the strength increases in as little as two weeks. Increases in muscle size take a little longer, but significant increases will become obvious within ten to fourteen weeks.

If I want to run and lift, is that okay? Running and lifting are commonly done together in an attempt to maintain or increase cardiovascular condition, increase strength, reduce injury and keep the body fit. As we have stated, each form of exercise will reduce the maximal level of performance possible in the other, unless the resistance training is done using low–intensity, high–duration patterns. Be careful in combining these exercises, since there is always the danger of overtraining when multiple exercise regimes are used.

How will I know if I am overtraining? Many athletes overtrain to force the body to make maximal adaptations when it recovers. This becomes counterproductive or even dangerous when the volume of training exceeds the body's ability to adapt. This can lead to poor performance, getting "stuck" at a specific training level, and in extreme cases, injury. Exercise professionals term this state "staleness." There are some signals which you should recognize:

- A lack of desire to work out. This may even reach levels of aggravation when the idea of going to the gym is mentioned, especially during the later stages of staleness;
- An increase of three or four beats per minute in your resting heart rate;
- Sleep disturbances, such as always being tired or being unable to sleep;
- Delayed recovery after a workout;
- Inability to complete your regular workout.

Although any of these events may occur occasionally, the appearance on a regular basis, or the combination of a number of these factors, may be a signal that the body is trying to tell you that you are overdoing it.

WEIGHT TRAINING AND GENDER

How do women compare to men physiologically? It is generally recognized that strength in women is approximately 50 to 60 percent that of men. The male advantage is due to several factors including anatomical and hormonal factors, greater size and less fatty tissue.

Endurance studies have shown that males have 10 to 12 percent more hemoglobin per milligram of blood and approximately eight percent more red blood cells per cubic centimeter. Men have larger hearts and lungs, slower heart rates, and ventilate less frequently during exercise. Women generally have 10 to 15 percent more body fat, which does provide more load on the cardiovascular system and offers more of a thermal barrier to the dissipation of body heat.

Studies do show that women's muscles can produce an equal amount of force per cross-sectional area as men's. However, men are usually larger and, therefore, stronger. The ability of women to produce equal force per muscles of equal size is especially evident when the lower body strengths of men and women are compared. They are much closer in leg size and strength.

How do growth patterns compare? Prior to puberty, there are few, if any, reasons for female performance to fall below that of males. However, beginning at about age eight, female performance on many motor tasks tends to lag behind that of males performing the same tasks. We also know that males tend to be stronger than females at all ages, and the increase in strength is about the same until 11 to 13 years of age. At this age, males significantly increase strength, while females maintain about the same rate of growth.

Males and females have approximately the same O_2 uptake until about age 12 to 13. At this age, males tend to increase much more rapidly. Females do not normally acquire the same level of work capacity as males at any age, and the difference increases greatly with age. Until approximately 11 years of age, proportional limb length is about the same. However, after age 11, limb length becomes greater for males than females. Additional differences in turning and jumping may be attributed to pelvic structure and the angle of the insertion of the femur into the pelvis. Body motion is sometimes described by positioning the center of mass. This is known to be lower in women, thus affording a more stable position for standing, running and walking. It is well–documented that men are generally stronger than women, and since the capacity to exert force is partially dependent upon the amount of muscle tissue at one's disposal, females are at a considerable disadvantage when competing with or against males.

What are the cultural implications of these difference? Play patterns of American boys and girls indicate the imposition of distinct patterns of play habits. Since this pattern has generally discouraged females from developing a strong sports background, research is not complete in this area. However, the results that have been collected tend to indicate the following:

1. Females participating in competitive athletics over a span of years appear to be as well–balanced psychologically as those who have not participated.
2. The level of performance is generally not affected by the menstrual period.
3. There is no evidence that childhood competitive sports affects the childbearing function of females.
4. Psychological stress in well–supervised programs is not likely to be harmful to young girls.
5. Girls of masculine–type build tend to be attracted to athletic competition, probably because of the success factor. However, there is no evidence to indicate that participation in athletics develops or contributes to masculinity.

As a female, how much can I expect to accomplish by taking up weight training? Since women are relatively new to this sport, we have limited knowledge. We do know, however, that female strength normally approximates about two–thirds that of male strength, and that females can respond to beginning weight training at approximately the same level as men. This means that women can significantly increase their strength by use of high–resistance exercise.

Can I lift weight without becoming "masculine" in appearance? The opposite occurs. A trim, firm, well–contoured figure is usually found among women who participate in regular exercise of this kind.

Dr. Lawrence E. Lamb, the noted medical expert, states: "A women can tighten her muscles and have attractive feminine curves with good strength (by practicing weight training) without fearing the development of what is classified as a more masculine physique."

As a female you have the same muscle properties as males; however, you do not have the same potential for developing muscular bulk and body size because of a hormone called testosterone, which is produced at a higher level in males. Conversely, males lack the hormone estrogen which is produced at a much higher level in women than in men. Men or women having an unusual amount of opposite hormone in their bodies will tend to display characteristics of the opposite sex. It is not the weight training that does it.

Do people of the same sex have the same potential for muscle size? Sorry about that, but your potential for muscular size is primarily influenced by the length of your muscles, and you didn't have much control over what you were given. Individuals who are blessed with longer muscle bellies have a greater potential for muscular size.

As a female do I have to vary my lifting pattern during my menstrual cycle? There is no indication that a woman must vary her lifting pattern during any phase of her menstrual cycle. In fact, it appears that regular exercise can even help to diminish discomfort due to menstruation.

WEIGHT TRAINING AND FOOD

Would "special foods" help me in my weight training program? Body builders are the world's worst when it comes to pouring exotic foods or potions into their systems. The only reason you should ever take special foods or additional vitamins is if you are not able to eat balanced meals, or if you are making weight for a sport and must stay on a low–calorie diet.

If you had to recommend just one vegetable as being the best all around for dietary eating, what would it be? If you want to get away from calories, a cup of chopped fresh broccoli fits the bill. For only 45 calories, you get about 200 percent of the daily requirement of vitamin C, about 25 percent of your daily fiber needs, about 90 percent of daily vitamin A needs, 10 percent each of calcium, phosphorous, and thiamin, and about eight percent of your daily protein requirement. Not bad for a cup of one vegetable! Some researchers also think broccoli is one of the vegetables that may protect us against certain forms of cancer.

Sometimes I lose large quantities of fluids due to heavy exercise. What is the best replacement and is there a rule of thumb for replacement? Endurance events lasting longer than 60 minutes will benefit more from a diluted (five to eight percent carbohydrate) drink because carbohydrates delay the beginning symptoms of exhaustion. The general rule of thumb is to drink fluids equal in volume to that lost by sweating. Sixteen fluid ounces are generally considered to be equal to one pound.

What do you think of soup as a dietary means of losing weight? An excellent means. One study at the University of Pennsylvania found that when people ate soup at the beginning of a meal, the stomach filled, which signalled the brain to curb appetites and slow the eating process. Other studies have found that dieters do better in losing and not regaining weight if they eat soup regularly.

Do "Energy Bars" boost or improve athletic performance? Energy bars, sport bars, power bars and nutrition bars are all typically high in calories, sugar and protein. Some may be touted as low fat, high fat, and/or fortified with a collection of minerals and vitamins. Others may contain totally useless ingredients such as ginseng or bee pollen.

It is a myth that eating a sugar snack prior to exercise will give you quick energy. While eating sugar does raise blood glucose levels and does provide some short–term release of energy, your body releases insulin, which ultimately may drop the blood glucose level lower than before you began. One exception is that if you are involved in a marathon–type workout lasting longer than two hours, you may delay the onset of fatigue by consuming a sugary snack.

Complex carbohydrates, on the other hand, are absorbed more slowly, and tend to have a more steady effect on the body's blood sugar. In most cases, stick with water and carbohydrates.

GENERAL QUESTIONS ABOUT WEIGHT TRAINING

NO
25%

Is the muscle very efficient in terms of calories consumed? Unfortunately this is not the case. When we do hard work, about 75 percent of the calories consumed are lost as body heat. The heart muscle is more efficient, converting 50 percent of its caloric fuel into effective work.

Why is weight training so much better at developing strength than just "playing" a sport or activity? Weight training equipment allows you to isolate the muscles surrounding a joint and to work them intensely. This selective overload provides you with more results in a few minutes than you might get in a week of playing the sport.

YES –
too
point

Can I become "faster" by using a weight training program? Speed is usually increased with the development of strength. However, there does seem to be a limit beyond which an additional increase in strength does not improve speed.

What about wrist straps? Are they helpful in lifting? Wrist straps have been around at least 30 to 40 years, and it is generally recognized that they do improve gripping ability. The advantages and disadvantages are:

Advantages:
Help to better isolate the primary muscles for each exercise.
Help prevent bars being dropped.
Give a psychological boost.
Allow lifters with faulty grips to compensate.

Disadvantages:
They are not permitted in competitive lifting.
Sometimes offer a false sense of security.
Lifter sometimes "goes with the bar" when a lift is missed.

I have several books on weight training. Is there anything that weight training experts agree on? While there are many divergent theories on weight training, most experts agree that muscular strength and growth are dependent upon:
  • Stimulation of muscle by high–intensity exercise to the point of fatigue.

- Rest 48–96 hours between sessions
- Proper nutrition
  Most also agree on the three principles of exercise, but not on the best way of achieving them. They are:
- Intensity—A degree of stimulation. Whatever that might be, it must be progressively greater than the normal workload of that person. This forces the body to adapt.
- Frequency—Or numbers of workouts. Most agree that 48–96 hours are needed to rebuild tissues.
- Duration—Somewhere between 30–60 minutes is most often recommended.

There also is agreement that both concentric and eccentric contraction are important. Concentric is the positive (tension and shortening) phase and eccentric is the negative (tension and lengthening) phase.

Are there any vitamins that are "Fat Burners"? No. Although some vitamins are necessary for the biochemical use of fat, as well as sugar and protein as a fuel, taking more of them will not increase fat utilization.

I have heard that a substance called Clembuterol will decrease body fat and increase strength. Anything to it? Clembuterol is a veterinary drug banned for use in America, but used on some animals outside the U.S. The real purpose of the drug is to increase muscle mass in show animals. It is not intended for human consumption. It has been reported that trace amounts of Clembuterol found in beef liver caused the hospitalization of 135 people in Spain.

Symptoms among the people contaminated by the drug in Spain were: muscular trembling, nausea, dizziness, fever, chills and headache. Clembuterol is clearly dangerous to humans and should not be used in any form.

Does steroid use continue to be a problem among athletes? Yes. Two recent studies found an average of nine percent of high school male athletes have used or presently use steroids in some form. This translates into nearly a half million athletes. Among males and student athletes at the college level, the numbers rise to 10–20 percent, despite all evidence of the hazardous physical and psychological side effects associated with continued usage of this substance.

Is there anything new on the advantages of a "warm-up" before engaging in physical exercise? Despite the scarcity of scientific evidence, most researchers continue to believe that a proper warm-up enhances performance and reduces the chance for injury. The chief reasoning behind this is that muscle activity raises muscle temperature, which in turn decreases the viscosity of the muscle. This reduces joint and muscle stiffness and increases range of motion.

What sport injuries are more common to women? Holly Atkinson, M.D. believes women are more prone to sport injuries than men, because they have less training and conditioning than the average male. She believes the three most prevalent injuries are: ankle sprain, lower back pain, and Achilles tendonitis. Among weight lifters, back pain is one of the more common complaints.

Is there a particular time of the day that seems to influence the number of injuries due to exercise? Dr. Richard Schuster, a noted exercise specialist, has reported that early morning runners developed more injuries than those who ran later in the day. He believes that early morning exercisers may tend to neglect or minimize stretching exercises or warm-ups. Another possible factor is that morning temperatures tend to be colder.

Are there different kinds or types of warm-ups? There are three methods of warming up: specific, general and passive.

A **specific** warm-up has at least two advantages. Not only does it increase the muscle temperature, but it also allows the body and mind to rehearse the movement and neural responses required for the forthcoming movement. This is generally considered to be the best type of warm-up.

The **general** warm-up involves the utilization of basic movement involving the major muscle groups. Examples would be jogging, rope jumping or cycling.

A **passive** warm-up involves such methods as hot baths, showers, massage or the use of heating pads. Present research indicates that these methods do not effectively increase muscle temperature. Another disadvantage is that excessive heat to the skin may draw a large amount of blood toward the skin, and away from the deep working muscles where it is needed.

12

Special Weight Training Programs

Throughout the text, we have attempted to explain the theory behind the manipulation of such variables as: number of reps per set, number of sets per workout, number of training days per week, speed of movement, and length of rest intervals. By now, you should have sufficient knowledge to create a personal lifting program. This final chapter is presented to offer examples of lifting programs for specific populations and competitive events.

TRAINING FOR COMPETITIVE ATHLETES

What is a competitive athlete? If you train and compete in road races, tennis leagues, softball leagues, triathlons, or any of the multitude of sports which are available to us, then you are a competitive athlete. Even though you may not be at the level of a professional, olympic, collegiate, or even high school competitor, you are still competing, and weight training can improve your performance. As we have stated, most informed coaches, exercise scientists, and athletes now accept the idea that resistance training provides a faster and better method of achieving success in sports or other activities than simple sports selective training. However, this is only true if the lifting program matches the specific sport.

In addition to matching specific lifting techniques to specific sports, the theory of periodization is important to the competitive athlete preparing for an event or competitive season.

Periodization

Periodization is a technique of changing the nature of the training relative to the time of the anticipated competition. The concept is based on the theory that training has three basic stages. The first stage is **overload**, when the muscles are stressed beyond their normal level of performance. The second stage is **adaptation**, where muscles change structure to adapt to the increase in stress. The final stage is **staleness**, where the muscles have made their adaptations and no longer respond to the previous training stimulus.

If an athlete repeats the same training stimulus, he will improve to a certain level, become stagnant, and ultimately fail to perform. Periodization changes the stimulus throughout the year, or a part of the year, so that changes in training encourage new adaptations by the body. In accomplishing this purpose, the athlete should peak at the time of the competition.

Classically, periodization has five separate phases to its cycle. Each stage increases in intensity and decreases in duration as the training continues. The idea is to move from a stage in which the muscle makes the necessary structural changes to allow it to handle the stresses (Phase 1) to a stage where the muscle begins to improve its strength (Phase 2). From this phase the intensity is raised by increasing both the weight and the speed of the activity (Phase 3). The final active phase (Phase 4) increases intensity to maximize stress and further stimulate the muscle toward even greater improvement. The last phase (Phase 5) involves minimal exercise (also called active rest) which is designed to allow the muscle to recover before competition. Table 12-1 provides a schematic of a 16-week periodization program.

As you can see from the chart, the phases use the same manipulation of reps and sets to dictate duration and intensity. In addition, the increases in speed of contraction (as well as weight)

PHASE	1	2	3	4	5
WEEK	Wks. 1-3	Wks. 4-6	Wks. 7-10	Wks. 11-13	Wks. 14-15
REPS	12-20	5-8	3-5	1-3	active rest
SETS	3-5	3-5	3-5	1-3	active rest

Table 12-1: Sixteen-week periodization program.

throughout the active training phases are designed to maximize the athlete's power for the competition. The athlete in the example in Table 12-1 is obviously a power athlete. The prescription for an endurance athlete would vary from this pattern by increasing the number of reps for all phases and reducing the number of sets.

Movement Specificity: Matching the Lift To The Sport

The training program should be designed to produce the greatest effects on those muscle groups most important to performance. Coaches now examine the movement pattern of their athletes to allow them to prescribe the proper speeds and intensities of movement for the proper muscles. For example, it would be a mistake to concentrate a large volume of training at heavy resistances on the upper body of a competitive road cyclist. This type of athlete does not require upper body strength or size. In fact, such a program would probably prove detrimental to the cyclist's performance.

The charts on the following pages show examples of sports-specific lifting programs that concentrate on the muscle groups used in a specific sport or activity. The recommendations given are for in–season training. This information does not include changes in lifts or training variables due to periodization, since it is beyond the scope of this text to present entire training programs for all sports. Following the sports programs are programs for working specific body parts, muscle tone, weight loss and gain, and circuit training.

NAME _____

Exercises: **BASEBALL IN SEASON—High Speed**									
	1		2		3		4		5
	Wt. Reps		Wt. Reps		Wt. Reps		Wt. Reps		Wt. Reps
Squat	5 RM		5 RM		5 RM				
Power Clean	5		5		5				
Leg Curl	8		8		8				
Bench Press	5		5		5				
Seated Row	8		8		8				
Incline Bench	5		5		5				
Behind Neck Press	8		8		8				
Lat Pulldown	8		8		8				
Triceps Ext.	5		5		5				
Bicep Curls	8		8		8				
Cross Crunch	50								

NAME _____

Exercises: **BASKETBALL (Guard)—High Speed**

	1 Wt.	Reps	2 Wt.	Reps	3 Wt.	Reps	4 Wt.	Reps	5 Wt.	Reps
Squat	5		5		5					
Power Clean	5		5		5					
Leg Abduction	8		8		8					
Leg Adduction	8		8		8					
Calf Raise	8		8		8					
Cross Crunch	10-15		10-15		10-15					
Leg Curl	15		15		15					
Triceps Ext.	8		8		8					
Biceps Curl	8		8		8					
Bench Press	8		8		8					

Exercises: **BASKETBALL (Forward)—High Speed**

	1 Wt.	Reps	2 Wt.	Reps	3 Wt.	Reps	4 Wt.	Reps	5 Wt.	Reps
Squat	5		5		5					
Power Clean	5		5		5					
Lat Pulldown	5		5		5					
Military Press	5		5		5					
Calf Raise	5		5		5					
Triceps Pulldown	5		5		5					
Leg Curl	10-15		10-15		10-15					
Cross Crunch	10-15		10-15		10-15					
Bent Lateral Raise	10		10		10					
Biceps Curl	8		8		8					
Bench Press	8		8		8					

NAME _____

Exercises: **CYCLING—High Speed**

	1 Wt.	1 Reps	2 Wt.	2 Reps	3 Wt.	3 Reps	4 Wt.	4 Reps	5 Wt.	5 Reps
Nautilus Hip		15-20		15-20		15-20				
Leg Ext.		15-20		15-20		15-20				
Leg Press		15-20		15-20		15-20				
Squats		8		8		8				
Leg Curls		15-20		15-20		15-20				
Crunches		25		25		25				
Wrist Curls		8-12		8-12		8-12				
Biceps Curls		8-12		8-12		8-12				
Triceps Ext.		8-12		8-12		8-12				
Bench Press		8-12		8-12		8-12				

NAME _____

Exercises: **GOLF—High Speed***

	1 Wt.	1 Reps	2 Wt.	2 Reps	3 Wt.	3 Reps	4 Wt.	4 Reps	5 Wt.	5 Reps
Lateral Raise		8		8		8				
Bent Over Lat. Raise*		8		8		8				
Seated Row		8		8		8				
Bench Press*		5		5		5				
Nautilus Rotary Torso		8		8		8				
Pec Deck*		8		8		8				
Triceps Pushdown		8		8		8				
Biceps Curl		10		10		10				
Wrist Curl		8		8		8				
Straight Leg Dead Lift		10		10		10				
Ab Crunches		25		25		25				

NAME _____

Exercises: VOLLEYBALL IN SEASON—High Speed Movements

	1 Wt.	1 Reps	2 Wt.	2 Reps	3 Wt.	3 Reps	4 Wt.	4 Reps	5 Wt.	5 Reps
Squat		5		5		5				
Power Clean		5		5		5				
Shoulder Press		8		8		8				
Triceps Pushdown		5		5		5				
Calf Raise		8		8		8				
Dumbbell Pullover		8		8		8				
Biceps Curl		8		8		8				
Leg Curl		8		8		8				
Cross Crunch		25		25		25				
Abdominal Crunch		50		50		50				

NAME _____

Exercises: TENNIS—High Speed*

	1 Wt.	1 Reps	2 Wt.	2 Reps	3 Wt.	3 Reps	4 Wt.	4 Reps	5 Wt.	5 Reps
Squat*		12		12		12				
Toe Raise		12		12		12				
Leg Curl		12		12		12				
Tricep Ext.*		8		8		8				
Arm Curl		12		12		12				
Wrist Curl		12		12		12				
Cross Crunches*		25		25		25				
Lateral Raise		8		8		8				
Ab Crunches*		30		30		30				

NAME _____

Exercises: **FOOTBALL (Linemen)—High Speed Movements**									
	1		**2**		**3**		**4**		**5**
	Wt.	Reps	Wt.	Reps	Wt.	Reps	Wt.	Reps	Wt.	Reps
Squat		5		5		5				
Power Clean		5		5		5				
Bench Press		5		5		5				
Seated Row		8		8		8				
Arm Curl		8		8		8				
Leg Curl		8		8		8				
Incline Bench		5		5		5				
Shrug/Upright Row		8		8		8				
Lat Pulldown		8		8		8				
Neck		8		8		8				
Lunges		5		5		5				
Dead Lift		8		8		8				
Wrist Curls		8		8		8				
Sit-ups		100								

NAME _____

Exercises: **GYMNASTICS**										
Monday	1 Wt.	Reps	2 Wt.	Reps	3 Wt.	Reps	4 Wt.	Reps	5 Wt.	Reps
Incline Bench		12		8						
Chin Ups		12								
N. Shoulder Press		12		8						
Tricep Pushdown		10		10						
Str. Bar Bicep		10		10						
Hip Sled		10		10						
Lunges		12								
Multi Toe Raises		10		10						
N. Leg Curl		10		10						
Crunch Machine		15								
Cycling–8:00										

Wednesday

	1		2		3		4		5	
N. Chest Press		12		8						
Nautilus Power		12		8						
Military Press		12		8						
Weighted Dips		10		10						
E–Z Bicep Curl		10		10						
Leg Extension		12		8						
Ab–Adductor		15								
Multi Toe Raises		10		10						
N. Leg Curl		10		10						
Weighted Sit–Ups		15								
Ball Throws		15								
Cycling–8:00										

Friday

	1		2		3		4		5	
Bench Press		12		8						
Close Grip Lat		12								
DB Lateral Raise		8		8						
Tricep Pushdown		12		8						
Manual Bicep		10								
N. Leg Press		12		8						
Hip Flexor		15								
Multi Toe Raises		10		10						
N. Leg Curl		10		10						
Cruch Machine		15								
Cycling–8:00										

NAME _____

Exercises: **HOCKEY IN SEASON**

Tuesday	1 Wt.	1 Reps	2 Wt.	2 Reps	3 Wt.	3 Reps	4 Wt.	4 Reps	5 Wt.	5 Reps
Bench Press		12		10		8				
Close Grip Lat		12		8						
Military Press		12		8						
Multi Ex Dips		10		10						
Str. Bar Bicep		10		10						
Hip Sled		10		8		8				
Lunges		12								
N. Leg Curl		10		10						
Crunch Machine		15								

Thursday

Thursday	Wt.	Reps	Wt.	Reps	Wt.	Reps	Wt.	Reps	Wt.	Reps
Incline Bench		10		8		8				
High Lat Pull		12		8						
N. Shoulder Press		12		8						
Tricep Pushdown		10		10						
E–Z Bicep Curl		10		10						
N. Leg Press		12		8						
Lunges		12								
N. Leg Curl		10		10						
Weighted Sit–Ups		15								

NAME _____

Exercises: **JOGGING—Free Weight & Universal**									
	1		**2**		**3**		**4**		**5**
	Wt.	Reps	Wt.	Reps	Wt.	Reps	Wt.	Reps	Wt.	Reps
Bench		10		10		10				
Dips		12								
Lateral Raises Dumbell		12								
Lat Pulldown		12								
Chin–Ups		12								
Reverse Curls		12								
Universal Leg Extension		15								
Universal Leg Press		15								
Universal Leg Curl		15								
Toe Raises		12		12		12				

NAME _____

Exercises: **LACROSSE**

Monday

	1 Wt.	1 Reps	2 Wt.	2 Reps	3 Wt.	3 Reps	4 Wt.	4 Reps	5 Wt.	5 Reps
Bench Press		7		5		4		3		2
High Lat Pull		10		8		6				
Military Press		10		8		6				
Tricep Pushdown		10		8		8				
E–Z Bicep Curl		10		8		6				
Back Squat		8		6		4		4		
Ab–Adductor		15								
Hip Sled Toe Raise		15		15						
N. Leg Curl		10		8		6				
Weighted Sit–Ups		15		15						

Wednesday

	Wt.	Reps	Wt.	Reps	Wt.	Reps	Wt.	Reps	Wt.	Reps
Incline Bench		7		5		5		3		
Chin–Ups		10		8		6				
N. Shoulder Press		15		10						
DB Lateral Raise		12								
Weighted Dips		15		10						
Manual Bicep Curl		12								
DB Bicep Curl		8		8						
Hip Sled		12		10		8				
Hip Flexer		15								
Hip Slet Toe Raise		15		15						
N. Leg Curl		15		10						
Roman Twist		15		10						

Friday

	Wt.	Reps	Wt.	Reps	Wt.	Reps	Wt.	Reps	Wt.	Reps
Bench Press		5		5		5		3		3
Close Grip Lat		12		10		8				
DB Lateral Raise		10		8						
Upright Row/Shrugs		15								
E–Z Tricep Press		10		8		8				
Str. Bar Bicep		10		10		10				
N. Leg Press		15		10						
Lunges		12								
Hip Sled Toe Raise		15		15						
N. Leg Curl		12		8						
Weighted Sit–Ups		15		15						

NAME _____

Exercises: **SKIING—Nautilus**

	1 Wt.	1 Reps	2 Wt.	2 Reps	3 Wt.	3 Reps	4 Wt.	4 Reps	5 Wt.	5 Reps
Hip & Back (Dupoly)		12								
Leg Extension		15								
Leg Curl		15								
Leg Press		15								
Chin–Ups		12								
Dips		12								
Shoulder Press		12								
Side Bend–Multi Ex.		15		15						
4–Way Neck		8–8		8–8						
Sit–Ups		23		23		23				

NAME _____

Exercises: **SKIING—Free Weight & Universal**

	1 Wt.	1 Reps	2 Wt.	2 Reps	3 Wt.	3 Reps	4 Wt.	4 Reps	5 Wt.	5 Reps
Squats		10		10		8		8		6
Stiff–Legged Deadlift		12								
Universal Leg Extension		15								
Universal Leg Curl		15								
Universal Leg Press		15								
Chin–Ups		12		8						
Dips		12		8						
Sitting Military		8		6						
Dumbell Side Bends		25		25						
Toe Raises		12		12		12				
Sit–Ups		25		25		25				

NAME _____

Exercises: **SOCCER IN SEASON—High Speed***									
	1 Wt. Reps		**2** Wt. Reps		**3** Wt. Reps		**4** Wt. Reps		**5** Wt. Reps
Squats*		10		10		10				
Leg Ext.		5		5		5				
Leg Curl		10		10		10				
Calf Raise		10		10		10				
Leg Abduction		5		5		5				
Leg Adduction*		8		8		8				
Cross Crunch*		25		25		25				
Lateral Raise		10		10		10				
Shrugs		10		10		10				
Neck		8		8		8				
Bench		10		10		10				
Triceps Ext.		10		10		10				
Biceps Curl		10		10		10				

NAME _____

Exercises: **SOFTBALL**										
	1		**2**		**3**		**4**		**5**	
Monday	Wt.	Reps	Wt.	Reps	Wt.	Reps	Wt.	Reps	Wt.	Reps
N. Chest Press		12		8						
Nautilus Pullover		12								
Military Press		12		8						
Weighted Dips		10		10						
Manual Bicep		10								
N. Leg Press		12		8						
Ab–Adductor		15								
N. Leg Curl		10		10						
Weighted Sit–Ups		15								
Wednesday										
Bench Press		12		8						
Close Grip Lat		12								
DB Lateral Raise		8		8						
Tricep Pushdown		12		8						
Str. Bar Bicep		10		10						
Hip Sled		10		10						
Hip Flexer		15								
N. Leg Curl		10		10						
Crunch Machine		15								
Friday										
Incline Bench		12		8						
Chin–Ups		12								
N. Shoulder Press		12		8						
Weighted Dips		10		10						
E–Z Bicep Curl		10		10						
Leg Extension		12		8						
Lunges		12								
N. Leg Curl		10		10						
Weighted Sit–Ups		15								

NAME _____

Exercises: **SWIMMING**										
	1		**2**		**3**		**4**		**5**	
Monday	Wt.	Reps	Wt.	Reps	Wt.	Reps	Wt.	Reps	Wt.	Reps
Bench Press		12		10		8				
High Lat Pull		12		8						
N. Shoulder Press		15		10						
Tricep Pushdown		12		8						
E–Z Bicep Curl		10		10						
Hip Sled		15		10						
Ab–Adductor		15								
Multi Toe Raises		15		15						
N. Leg Curl		12		8						
Crunch Machine		15								
Ball Throws		15		15						
Wednesday										
Military Press		10		10		10				
Chin–Ups		12		8						
Bench Press		8		8		8				
E–Z Tricep Press		10		10						
Str. Bar Bicep		12		8						
N. Leg Press		15		10						
Multi Toe Raises		15		15						
N. Leg Curl		10		10						
Weighted Sit–Ups		15		15						
Ball Throws		15		15						
Friday										
Incline Bench		10		8		8				
E–Z Pullover		10		10						
Upright Row/Shrugs		10		10						
Weighted Dips		15		10						
Manual Bicep		8								
Hip Sled		10		10						
Hip Flexer		15								
Multi Toe Raises		15		15						
N. Leg Curl		12		8						
Crunch Machine		15								
Ball Throws		15		15						

NAME _____

Exercises: **TRACK IN SEASON**

Tuesday	1 Wt.	Reps	2 Wt.	Reps	3 Wt.	Reps	4 Wt.	Reps	5 Wt.	Reps
Bench Press		12		10		8				
Chin–Ups		12		8						
Military Press		12		8						
Multi Ex Dips		10		10						
Str. Bar Bicep		10		10						
Hip Sled		10		8		6				
Hip Flexer		15								
Lunges		12								
Multi Toe Raises		15		15						
N. Leg Curl		10		10						
Crunch Machine		15								

Thursday

	1 Wt.	Reps	2 Wt.	Reps	3 Wt.	Reps	4 Wt.	Reps	5 Wt.	Reps
Incline Bench		10		8		8				
High Lat Pull		12		8						
N. Shoulder Press		12		8						
Tricep Pushdown		10		10						
E–Z Bicep Curl		10		10						
Back Squat		12		8						
Ab-Adductor		15								
Lunges		12								
Multi Toe Raises		15		15						
N. Leg Curl		10		10						
Weighted Sit–Ups		15								

NAME _____

Exercises: **WRESTLING**										
Monday	**1** Wt.	Reps	**2** Wt.	Reps	**3** Wt.	Reps	**4** Wt.	Reps	**5** Wt.	Reps
Bench Press		8		6		4		4		
High Lat Pull		12		10		8				
DB Lateral Rise		12		8						
Tricep Pushdown		10		10		10				
E–Z Bicep Curl		10		10		10				
Back Squat		10		8		6				
Ab–Adductor		15								
N. Leg Curl		15		10						
Crunch Machine		15		10						

Wednesday										
Incline Bench		10		8		6		4		
Chin–Ups		15		10						
N. Shoulder Press		12		8						
Weighted Dips		15		10						
Manual Bicep Curl		12		8						
N. Leg Press		12		8						
Hip Flexer		15								
N. Leg Curl		15		10						
Weighted Sit–Ups		15		10						

Friday										
Bench Press		10		8		6		4		
E–Z Pullover		10		10		10				
Military Press		10		8		6				
Upright Row/Shrugs		12		8						
E–Z Tricep Press		10		10		10				
Str. Bar Bicep		10		10		10				
Hip Sled		15		10						
Lunges		12								
N. Leg Curl		15		10						
Crunch Machine		15		10						

NAME _____

Exercises: **CHEST DEVELOPMENT—Nautilus**

	1 Wt.	Reps	2 Wt.	Reps	3 Wt.	Reps	4 Wt.	Reps	5 Wt.	Reps
Chest Uppers–Positive		12								
Chest Press–Positive		12								
Multi Ex Dips–Negative		12								
10° Angle Chest		12								
40° Angle Chest		12								

NAME _____

Exercises: **CHEST DEVELOPMENT—Free Weight & Universal**

	1 Wt.	Reps	2 Wt.	Reps	3 Wt.	Reps	4 Wt.	Reps	5 Wt.	Reps	6 Wt.	Reps
Bench Press		8		6		6		4		4		
Incline Bench		8		6		4						
Dumbbell Chest Flys		12		8								
Dumbbell Chest Press		12		8								
Weighted Dips		12		8								
Bent–Over Rowing		12		8								
Push–Ups		10		9		8		7		6		5

NAME _____

Exercises: **HIPS—Free Weight & Universal**

	1 Wt.	1 Reps	2 Wt.	2 Reps	3 Wt.	3 Reps	4 Wt.	4 Reps	5 Wt.	5 Reps
Squats		10		10		10		8		8
Universal Leg Press		15								
Universal Leg Extension		15								
Universal Leg Curl		15								
Side Leg Raises		15		15						
Crunches		12								
Step–Ups		20		15						
Universal Ab-Adductor		25		25						
Side Bends		25		25						
Sit–Ups		25								

NAME _____

Exercises: **WEIGHT LOSS—Free Weight & Universal**

	1		2		3		4		5	
	Wt.	Reps	Wt.	Reps	Wt.	Reps	Wt.	Reps	Wt.	Reps
Bench		12		12		12				
Dumbbell Chest Flys		18								
Dumbbell Lat Raises		18								
Lateral Pulldown		18								
Dumbbell Side Bends		18		18						
Universal Leg Extension		18								
Universal Leg Press		18								
Universal Leg Curl		18								
Low Pulley Lat Raises		18		18						
Sit–Ups		50								
Jump Rope		5 mins.								

NAME _____

Exercises: **WEIGHT GAIN—Free Weight & Universal**

	1		2		3		4		5	
	Wt.	Reps	Wt.	Reps	Wt.	Reps	Wt.	Reps	Wt.	Reps
Bench		6		4		2		1		
Dumbbell Incline		8		6		4				
Sitting Military		8		6		4				
High Pull		8		6		4				
Biceps/Curls		8		6						
Triceps Ext.		8		6						
Squats		8		6		4				
Universal Leg Extension		15								
Universal Leg Press		15								
Universal Leg Curl		15								

NAME _____

Exercises: **MUSCLE TONE—Free Weight & Universal**

	1 Wt.	1 Reps	2 Wt.	2 Reps	3 Wt.	3 Reps	4 Wt.	4 Reps	5 Wt.	5 Reps	6 Wt.	6 Reps
Bench		10		8		8		8		6		4
Dumbell Incline Press		12										
Dumbbell Lateral Raises		12										
Sitting Military		12										
Lateral Pulldown		12										
Pull–Ups		12										
Triceps Ext.		12										
Biceps Curls		12										
Universal Leg Extension		15										
Universal Leg Press		15										
Universal Leg Curls		15										

NAME _____

Exercises: **CIRCUIT TRAINING**										*30 sec. rest between set and station
	1		**2**		**3**		**4**		**5**	
	Wt.	Reps	Wt.	Reps	Wt.	Reps	Wt.	Reps	Wt.	Reps
Bench		10		8		6				
High Pulls		10		8		6				
Leg Extension		10		8		6				
Leg Curl		10		8		6				
Sit–Ups		10		8		6				
Military Press		10		8		6				
AMF Leg Press		10		8		6				
Lat Pulldown		10		8		6				
Dips		10		8		6				
Jump Rope		60		60		60				

NAME _____

Exercises: **HEAVY CIRCUIT**										
	1		**2**		**3**		**4**		**5**	
	Wt.	Reps	Wt.	Reps	Wt.	Reps	Wt.	Reps	Wt.	Reps
Bench Press		8		6		4				
Power Pulls		8		6		4				
Squats		8		6		4				
Military Press		8		6		4				
AMF Leg Press		8		6		4				
Leg Curl		15		10						

SPECIAL CONSIDERATIONS FOR OLDER LIFTERS

For years, many health professionals have considered high–intensity weight training as too stressful for persons over 60 years of age. There were fears of muscle tears, tendinitis, broken bones, and shredded connective tissue. Fortunately, considerable research has shown that these myths are no longer accepted by the sports medicine community. Experts in the field currently believe that resistance training is as important as cardiovascular training for the older population.

The prevention of dehabilitating falls has been directly correlated with increases in leg strength. Most of the activities of daily living that become difficult for the elderly, can be made easier by a well–designed weight training program. Some of the most recent studies have documented strength gains of over 20–30 percent in patients as old as 90 years or more. To put this in perspective, it has been estimated by some researchers that an elderly person may require over 120 percent of his or her leg strength to rise from a chair. Weight training can allow a person to perform this simple act unassisted, by pushing with the arms. At a time when our nation is about to experience the "graying of America," it is important that our older citizens be given every opportunity to maintain personal levels of activity and independence. Weight training is one of the most powerful tools available to reach these goals.

The goals of older individuals can been summarized in a simple statement: progressive increases in strength and speed of motion, to counteract the loss of strength, speed and muscle tissue which accompanies old age. What follows is information that should be considered as you grow older.

First, a thorough physical should precede any program intended to increase an individual's level of activity to the degree that weight training will stress all systems of the body. The physical should include an evaluation of the cardiovascular system, musculoskeletal system, nervous system, and all endocrine functions.

Second, all lifting sessions should be preceded by a 25–30 minute warm–up which includes: low–intensity aerobic exercise to warm up the muscles, joints, and connective tissue, and a series of muscle specific stretches which concentrate on the specific muscles to be trained.

Third, low–intensity exercise should be used at the beginning of the program. The central nervous system improves its ability to "fire" the muscles long before the muscles themselves hypertrophy, or the connective tissue thickens sufficiently to handle the stress. Since there may be a slight loss in tissue compliancy with age, and repair of damaged tissue is definitely slower, low weights should be used for at least the first two weeks with slow increases in weight until an 8–12 rep figure is reached.

Fourth, the beginning movements should concentrate heavily on the lower body, since the legs and hips constitute the major controls of balance. Exercises should be added until a full body workout is developed. Overhead exercises such as the military press are also quite helpful since they add stress to the muscles of the back.

Finally, added safety and control can be provided by using machines for the workout. These machines should be examined to ensure the lifter can get in and out with relative ease.

Below is a typical full body machine workout.

NAME **OLDER LIFTERS (60+)**

Exercises: NAUTILUS

	1 Wt.	1 Reps	2 Wt.	2 Reps	3 Wt.	3 Reps	4 Wt.	4 Reps	5 Wt.	5 Reps
Leg Press		8-10 RM		8-10 RM		8-10 RM				
Leg Extension		8-10		8-10		8-10				
Leg Curl		8-10		8-10		8-10				
Overhead Press		8-10		8-10		8-10				
Lat Pullover		8-10		8-10		8-10				
Biceps Curl		8-10		8-10		8-10				
Triceps Ext.		8-10		8-10		8-10				

WOMEN AND STRENGTH TRAINING

As we have stated, there has been a stigma attached to weight training for women that has falsely centered around the notion that weight training will cause a woman to become masculine. There are a number of strong arguments that contradict this myth.

The first, and possibly the most convincing argument has to do with the "ideal feminine form" on which this myth is based. We need only look at the sculptures and paintings throughout the ages to realize that the ideal feminine form has undergone transitions. There is no true ideal feminine form, only the artificial dictates of society.

The second argument against this myth of defeminization is that it is extremely difficult, and for most women, impossible, for the female body to gain the same level of mass as males. This is due to differences in the levels of hormones. The androgens (male hormones), which allow males to develop greater mass, are at such low levels in females that they cannot produce the same mass as males without anabolic steroids.

Third, that a woman chooses to play a certain sport, finds a specific body type more desirable, or would rather be in the gym than in the sewing room, is no indication of her sexuality. The concept of the male as a doer, and the female as a passive spectator is outdated.

There are a number of other considerations that should be addressed concerning women and lifting. The first concerns the impact of lifting on the menstrual cycle. There are considerable data that correlate changes in the regularity of the menstrual cycle with high–intensity training and extreme reductions in body fat. While this is not reported by all women, it can occur. These changes are reversible with changes in the intensity of the work-out. Any change, however, in the regularity of the menstrual cycle should be reported and discussed with a physician.

An additional question concerning the menstrual cycle and lifting is whether it will increase menstrual pain. All reports indicate the opposite. Female athletes actually report less menstrual pain than non–exercising women.

Finally, the question often arises, should women train differently than men? No. Muscle will adapt to the training stimulus applied. Women should incorporate the same training principles as men.

As with older participants, the use of high–intensity overhead lifts is recommended for women. These lifts increase exercise stress on the spine and its related musculature. It is especially important for women to consider this since the spine is the area most affected by osteoporosis.

STRENGTH TRAINING FOR CHILDREN

Much has been written concerning the potential for injury as a result of weight training in adolescent and prepubescent children. These concerns include damage to the growth plates and subsequent stunted or contorted growth, damage to the developing cartilage in the joints, and damage where the tendon attaches to the bone. These areas are especially susceptible to damage in children since they contain a large proportion of undeveloped cartilage–like tissue that is constantly making new cells. The tissue must be soft at first to allow for increases in size, and with aging, it becomes ossified (hardened by the addition of calcium, magnesium, and other minerals) to increase its strength. Since the growth plates and tendon and ligament insertions are constantly undergoing this process during the development of the child, these areas of relative weakness are constant, and the chain is always damaged at its weakest link. Weight training causes changes in strength and size by placing considerable external force on the body to promote an adaptation. Therefore, it would seem reasonable that these stresses could damage those softer growing areas of the child's skeleton causing permanent problems.

While this fear is warranted, it is not a reason to avoid weight training. In fact, it may be the recognition of the potential for injury during weight training that has kept the level of injury to a minimum. Weight training injuries in children usually involve one or more of the following situations:

1. Maximal lifting, especially overhead;
2. Unsupervised or poorly supervised lifting involving poor form, poor or no spotting, incorrect loads.
3. Horseplay in the weight room.

For these reasons we make the following recommendations for young lifters:

1. Never lift without adult supervision. In addition, that adult should be someone who is not only well–versed in proper

weight training techniques, but also knowledgeable about their applications to a younger population.

2. Never attempt a maximal lift, especially an overhead lift.
3. Practice all lifts with no weight to ensure that proper form is used *before* attempting the actual exercise.
4. Avoid ballistic movements that may place added stresses on the bones and connective tissue.
5. Emphasize the importance of weight room safety, including proper footwear, no horseplay, and proper spotting techniques.

The current data available indicates that weight training is one of the safest activities in which children can participate, as long as these safety guidelines are met. But, lifting without proper instruction and supervision can cause serious if not permanent damage.

Appendix A: Bibliography

Periodicals

Aniansson, A., Grimby, G., and Hedberg, M. (1992). *J. Appl. Physio.,* 73(3):812–816.

Aniansson, A.C., Zitterberg, C., and Hedberg, M. et al. (1984). Impaired muscle function with aging: a background factor in the incidence of fractures of the proximal end of the femur. *Clin. Orthop. Rel. Res.,* 191:193–210.

Aniansson, A., Sperling, L., Rundgren, A., and Lehnberg, E. (1983). Muscle function in 75 year old men and women: a longitudinal study. *Scand. J. Rehab. Med. (Suppl)* 9:92–102.

Baker, S.P. and Harvey, A.H. (1985). Fall injuries in the elderly. *Clin. Geriatr. Med.,* 1:501–512.

Bomze, J.P. and Miles, D.S. (1991). A historical and clinical perspective. *NSCA Journal,* 13(5):42–46.

Congressional Budget Office (March 1988). *Changes in the living arrangements of the elderly: 1960–2030.*

Corbin, Charles B. and Pangrazzi, R.P. (1992). Are American Children and Youth Fit? (1992). *Research Quarterly for Exercise and Sport,* 63(2):96–106.

Cordes, K. (1991). Reasons to strength train for amateur boxing. *NSCA Journal,* 13(5):18–21.

Department of Health and Human Resources, Administration on Aging. (August 1989). *The needs of the elderly in the 21st century.* Washington D.C.:Urban Institute.

Effron, M.B. (1989). Effects of resistive training on left ventricular function. *Sci. Med. Sports & Exercise,* 21(6):694–697.

Essen-Gustavsson, B. and Borges, O. (1986). Histochemical and metabolic characteristics of human skeletal muscle in relation to age. *Acta Physiol. Scand.,* 126:107–114.

Ewart, C.K. (1989). Psychological effects of resistive weight training: implications for cardiac patients. *Med. Sci. Sports & Exercise,* 21(6): 683–688.

Fiatarone, M.A. and Evans, W.J. (1990). *Topics in Geriatric Rehabilitation,* 5(2):63–77.

Fiatarone, M.A., Marks, E.C., Ryan, D.T., Meredith, C.N., Lipsitz, L.A., and Evans, W.J. (1990). High intensity training in nonagenarians, *JAMA,* 263(22):3029–3034.

Field, R.W. (1988). Rationale for the use of free weights for periodization. *NSCA Journal,* 10(2):38–42.

Fontera, W.A., Meredith, C.N., O'Reilly, K.P., Knittgen, H.G., and Evans, W.J. (1988). Strength conditioning in older men: skeletal muscle hypertrophy and improved function. *J. Appl. Physiol.,* 64:1038–1044.

Goldberg, A.P. (1989). Aerobic and resistive exercise modify risk factors for coronary heart disease. *Med. Sci. Sports & Exercise,* 21(6):669–674.

Gryfe, C.I., Amies, A., and Ashley, M.J. (1977). A longitudinal study of falls in an elderly population. I. Incidence and morbidity. *Age Aging,* 6:201–210.

Hurley, B.F. (1989). Effects of resistive on lipoprotein–lipid profiles: a comparison to aerobic exercise training. *Med. Sci. Sports & Exercise,* 21(6):689–693.

Jette, A.M. and Branch, L.G. (1981). The Framingham disability study:II. Physical disability among the aging *American Journal of Public Health,* 71:1211–1216.

Kelemen, M.H. (1989). Resistive training safety and assessment guidelines for cardiac and coronary prone patients. *Med. Sci. Sports & Exercise,* 21(6):675–677.

Kohl III, H.W., Gordon, N.F., Scott, C.B. Vaandrager, H., and Blair, S.N. (1992). Musculoskeletal strength and serum lipid levels in men and women. *J Appl. Physiol.,* 24(10):1080–1087.

Kokkinos, P.F., Hurley, B.F., Smutok, M.A., Farmer, C., Reece, C., Shulman, R., Charabogos, C., Patterson, J., Will, S., Devane–Bell, J., and Goldberg, A.P. *Med Sci Sports and Exercise,* 23(10):1134–1139.

Kuntzleman, C.T. and Reiff, G.G. (1992). The Decline in American Children's Fitness Levels. *Research Quarterly for Exercise and Sport,* 63(2):107-111.

Lamb, D.R. and Brodowicz, G.R. (1986). Optimal Use of Fluids of Varying Formulations to Minimize Exercise-Induced Disturbances in Homeostasis. *ADIS Press Limited,* 3:247–274.

Lemon, P.W.R., Tarnopolsky, M.A., MacDougall, J.D., and Atkinson, S.A. (1992). Protein requirements and mass/strength changes during intensive training in novice bodybuilders. *J. Appl. Physiol.,* 73(2):393–404.

Marcinik, E.J., Potts, G., Schlabach, G., Will, S., Dawson, P. and Hurley, B.F. (1990). Effects of strength training on lactate threshold and endurance performance. *Med. Sci. Sports & Exercise,* 23(6):739–743.

Millard-Stafford, M. (1992). Fluid Replacements During Exercise in the Heat. *Sports Medicine,* 13(4):225–233.

National Strength and Conditioning Association (1989). Strength training for female athletes: A position paper: Part II. *NSCA Journal,* 11(5):29–37.

Nevitt, M.C., Cummings, S.R., Kidd, S., and Black, D. (1989). Risk factors for recurrent nonsyncopal falls: a prospective study. *JAMA,* 261:2663–2668.

Palmieri, G.A. (1983). The principles of muscle fiber recruitment applied to strength training. *NSCA Journal,* 5(5):22–25.

Pauletto, B. (1986). Periodization—Peaking. *NSCA Journal,* 8(4):30–31.

Peterson, S.E., Peterson, M.D., Raymond, G., Gilligan, C., Checovich, M.M. and Smith, E.L. (1991). Muscular strength and bone density with weight training in middle–aged women. *Med. Sci. Sports & Exercise,* 23(4):499–504.

Ramsay, J.A., Blimkie, J.R., Smith, K., Garner, S., MacDougall, J.D. and Sale, D.G. (1990). Strength training effects in prepubescent boys. *Med. Sci. Sports & Exercise,* 22(5):605–614.

Rubenstein, L., Robbins, A., Josephson, K., Schulman, B., Fine, G., Osterweil, D., and Kornbluth, A. (1988). Predictors of falls in an institutional elderly population: results of a case-control study, abstracted. *J. Am. Geriatr. Soc.,* 36:578.

Schafer, J. (1991). Prepubescent and adolescent weight training: Is it safe? Is it beneficial? *NSCA Journal,* 13(1):39–46.

Shepherd, R.J., and Leat, P. (1987). Carbohydrate and Fluid Needs of the Soccer Player. *Sports Medicine,* 4:164–176.

Smith, E.L., Gilligan, M., McAdam, M., Ensign, C.P. and Smith, P.E. (1989). Deterring bone loss by exercise intervention in premenopausal and postmenopausal women. *Calcif. Tissue Int.,* 44:312–321.

Stewart, K.J. (1989). Resistive training effects on strength and cardiovascular endurance in cardiac and coronary prone patients. *Med. Sci. Sports and Exercise,* 21(6):678–682.

The prevention of falls in later life: a report of the Kellogg International Work Group on the Prevention of Falls by the Elderly (1987). *Dan. Med. Bull,* 34(Suppl 4):1–24.

Three periods of the snatch and clean and jerk (1989). *NSCA Journal,* 10(6):33–40.

Tinetti, M.E. (1987). Factors associated with serious injury during falls by ambulatory nursing home residents. *J. Am. Geriatr. Soc.,* 35:644.

Tomonaga, M. (1977). Histochemical and ultrastructural changes in senile human skeletal muscle. *J. Am. Geriatr. Soc.,* 25(3):125–131.

Training the older athlete. Part II—Practical Considerations. *NSCA Journal,* 10(6):10–14.

Water–Storer, C.M. (1991). The cytoskeleton of skeletal muscle: is it affected by exercise? *Med. Sci. Sports and Exercise,* 1240–1249.

Wheeler, K.B., and Banwell, J.G. (1986). Intestinal water and electrolyte flux of glucose-polymer electrolyte solutions. *Med. and Sci in Sports & Exercise,* 18(4):436–439.

Young, A. (1987) Exercise physiology in geriatric practice. *Acta. Med. Scand.,* 711:227–232.

Young, W. (1991). The planning of resistance training for power sports. *NSCA Journal,* 13(4):26–29.

Zatsiorsky, V.M. and Central Institute of Physical Culture (1992). *NSCA Journal,* 14(5):40–41.

Textbooks

Alter, M.J. (1988). *Science of Stretching.* Champaign: Human Kinetics Books.

Enoka, R.M. (1988). *Neuromechanical Basis of Kinesiology.* Champaign: Human Kinetics Books.

Fleck, S.J. and Kraemer, W.J. (1992). *Designing Resistance Training Programs.* Human Kinetics Publishers, Inc.

Fox, E.L. Bowers, R.W. and Foss, M.L. (1988). *The Physiological Basis of Physical Education and Athletics.* Philadelphia: Saunders College Publishing.

Gray, H. (1957). *Anatomy, Descriptive and Surgical.* New York: Bounty Books.

Gowitzbe, B.A. and Milner, M. (1988). *Scientific Bases of Human Movement.* Baltimore: Williams and Wilkins.

Hatfield, F.C and Krotee, M. (1984). *Personalizes Weight Training for Fitness and Athletics: From Theory to Practice.* Dubuque: Kendall/Hunt Publishing Company.

Hays J.G. (1973). *The Biomechanics of Sports Techniques.* Englewood Cliffs: Prentice–Hall Incorporated.

Jones, N.L., McCartney, N., and McComas, A.J. ed. (1986). *Human Muscle Power.* Champaign: Human Kinetics Publishers.

Komi, P.V. ed. (1992). *Strength and Power in Sports.* London: Blackwell Scientific Publications.

Lieber, R.L. (1992). *Skeletal Muscle Structure and Function.* Baltimore: Williams and Wilkins.

MacDougall, J.D., Wenger, H.A., and Green, H.J. (1992). *Physiological Testing of the High-Performance Athlete.*

Sieg, K.W. and Adams, S.P. (1985). *Illustrated Essentials of Musculoskeletal Anatomy.* Gainesville: Megabooks.

Squire, J.M. ed.(1990). *Molecular Mechanisms in Muscular Contraction.* Boca Raton: CRC Press Incorporated.

Sutton, J.R. and Brock, R.M. (1986). *Sports Medicine for the Mature Athlete.* Indianapolis: Benchmark Press.

Taylor, A.W., Gollnick, P.D., Green, H.J., Ianuzzo, C.D., Noble, E.G., Metivier, G., and Sutton, J.R. (1990). *Biochemistry of Exercise VII.* Champaign: Human Kinetics Books.

Appendix B: Kilo/Pound Conversion Table

Kilos are converted to pounds by multiplying by 2.2046. A.A.U. weightlifting rules stipulate that pounds shall be rounded off by reducing to the nearest quarter pound. For example: 120 kilos multiplied by 2.2046 = 264.552. This translates to 264.5 pounds.

Kilos	Pounds	Kilos	Pounds	Kilos	Pounds
5	11	197.5	435.25	297.5	655.75
10	22	200	440.75	300	661.25
15	33	202.5	446.25	302.5	666.75
20	44	205	451.75	305	672.25
25	55	207.5	457.25	307.5	677.75
30	66.25	210	462.75	310	683.25
35	77.25	212.5	468.25	312.5	688.75
40	88.25	215	473.75	315	694.25
45	99.25	217.5	479.5	317.5	699.75
50	110.25	220	485	320	705.25
55	121.25	222.5	490.5	322.5	710.75
60	132.25	225	496	325	716.25
65	143.5	227.5	501.5	327.5	722
70	154.5	230	507	330	727.5
75	165.5	232.5	512.5	332.5	733
80	176.5	235	518	335	738.5
85	187.5	237.5	523.5	337.5	744
90	198.5	240	529	340	749.5
95	209.5	242.5	534.5	342.5	755
100	220.5	245	540	345	760.5
105	231.5	247.5	545.5	347.5	766
110	242.5	250.0	551	350	771.5
115	253.5	252.5	556.5	352.5	777
120	264.5	255	562	355	782.5
125	275.5	257.5	567.5	357.5	788
130	286.5	260	573	360	793.5
135	297.5	262.5	578.5	362.5	799
140	308.75	265	584	365	804.5
145	319.75	267.5	589.5	367.5	810
150	330.75	270	595	370	815.5
155	341.75	272.5	600.75	372.5	821
160	352.75	275	606.25	375	826.5
165	363.75	277.5	611.75	377.5	832
170	374.75	280	617.25	380	837.5
175	385.75	282.5	622.75	382.5	843.25
180	396.75	285	628.25	385	848.75
185	407.75	287.5	633.75	387.5	854.25
187.5	413.25	290	639.25	390	859.75
190	418.75	292.5	644.75	392.5	865.25
192.5	424.25	295	650.25	395	870.75
195	429.75				

Appendix C: Muscles of the Body

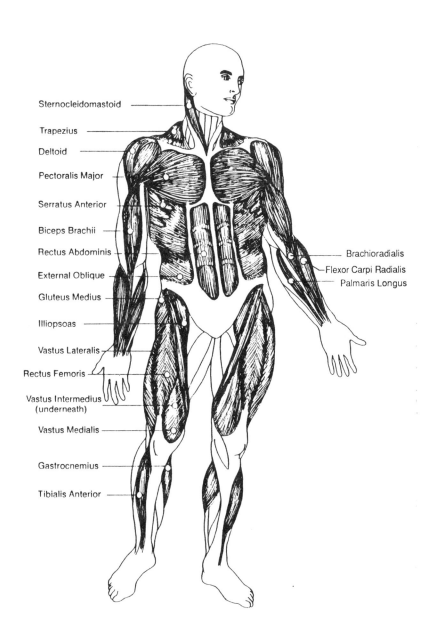

Sternocleidomastoid

Trapezius

Deltoid

Pectoralis Major

Serratus Anterior

Biceps Brachii

Rectus Abdominis

External Oblique

Gluteus Medius

Illiopsoas

Vastus Lateralis

Rectus Femoris

Vastus Intermedius (underneath)

Vastus Medialis

Gastrocnemius

Tibialis Anterior

Brachioradialis

Flexor Carpi Radialis

Palmaris Longus

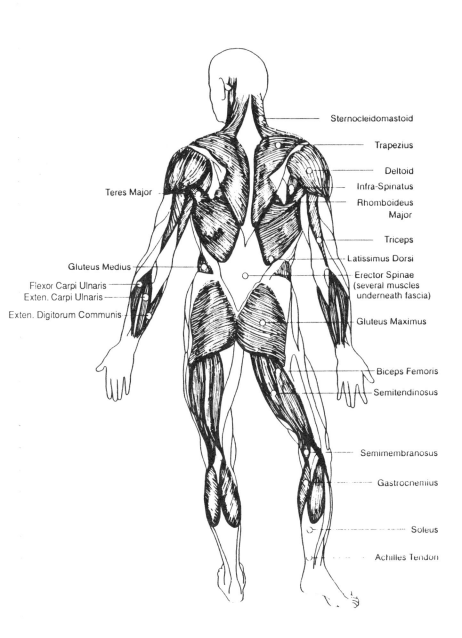

Sternocleidomastoid

Trapezius

Deltoid

Infra-Spinatus

Rhomboideus
Major

Triceps

Latissimus Dorsi

Erector Spinae
(several muscles
underneath fascia)

Gluteus Maximus

Biceps Femoris

Semitendinosus

Semimembranosus

Gastrocnemius

Soleus

Achilles Tendon

Teres Major

Gluteus Medius

Flexor Carpi Ulnaris

Exten. Carpi Ulnaris

Exten. Digitorum Communis

Appendix D: Common Body Building Measurements

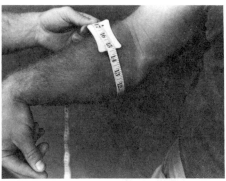

Forearm measurement.
Flex the arm so that forearm muscles are fully contracted, with the arm straight and pointing away from the body. Measure at the point of greatest girth below the elbow.

Biceps measurement
Bend the arm so that upper arm muscles are fully contracted. Measure at the highest peak of muscle.

Shoulder Girdle measurement
Place the tape approximately one inch below tip of shoulder and measure entire circumference of body including the opposite shoulder.

Normal chest measurement.
The head is up and body erect with normal breathing; the tape should be placed slightly above the nipples and straight around the body. Be certain that the latissimus dorsi muscles are fully relaxed.

Expanded chest measurement .
Place the tape in the same position as for measuring the normal chest. Inhale as deeply as possible, taking care to not contract the latissimus dorsi muscles. If the expansion measurement exceeds the normal measurement by 2 or 3 inches, it should be retaken.

Neck measurement
The head is up, eyes forward and neck muscles relaxed. Carefully take the measurement at the smallest circumference which will be slightly above the Adam's apple.

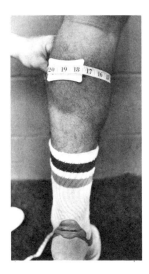

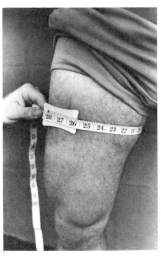

Calf measurement
Standing erect and with weight equally distributed on both legs, measure at the largest girth, or about four inches below the knee joint.

Thigh measurement
Standing erect with feet 6 to 8 inches apart with the thigh muscles relaxed, measure at the greatest girth.

Waist measurement
Standing erect and relaxed, place the tape slightly above the navel, and be certain to not suck in the abdomen.

Appendix E: Sample Examination

Part I: True or False

F   1. One drawback of weight training is the extremely high cost of the equipment needed. *moderate cost*

F   2. The overload principle states that if you overload your muscles they will be injured causing damage. *they'll improve*

T   3. A muscle, such as the biceps brachii, is composed of thousands of thread–like muscle fibers.

T   4. The intensity of a weight training exercise can be directly affected by the amount of weight you lift.

F   5. The two proteins which interact during muscle contraction are myosin and hemoglobin. *myosin & actin*

F   6. Hypertrophy and hyperplasia mean exactly the same thing, muscle growth. *hypertrophy - add proteins to enlarge* *hyperplasia - make new fiber*

F   7. Bones are attached to bones by tendons. *by ligaments*

F   8. Although muscle grows when exercised, bone is mineralized and cannot grow. *bone grows too*

T   9. Adduction is the movement of a body part toward the midline of the body.

F   10. Since the human body is a series of bony levers, it can be argued that the human body is built for strength. *built for movement*

T   11. An isokinetic contraction is one where the speed of the movement is held constant.

T   12. Since many machines dictate the path of motion of the weight, there is less development of accessory muscles than using free weights. *squat, bench, dumbbells*

p. 29

F   13. Spotters are necessary for all free weight lifts.

F   14. The Universal was one of the first, and most successful, multi–purpose isokinetic machines.

T   15. One of the advantages of machines is the ease of changing resistance.

T   16. Strength refers to the maximal amount of weight an individual can lift.

T   17. The lower the RM figure the more intense the exercise.

F   18. The most effective way to develop power is by using slow deliberate movements. *power involves speed*

F   19. "Mirror Consciousness" is the best way to evaluate your muscles and decide on a proper workout.

F   20. One of the best ways to improve your squat is to run long distances to increase leg size and strength.

F 21. Since weight training is not an aerobic exercise, it is okay to smoke and lift.

see 161 True 22. Fitness in American children has been on the decline since 1960.

F 23. Protein supplements are an absolute necessity for the weight trainer since increases in muscle size are caused by increased protein.

T 24. The recommended percentage of body fat for a college–aged male is between 12 and 15 percent.

T 25. Power is nothing more than a measurement of the speed at which work is done.

62 True 26. The squat and power clean are multi–joint exercises usually employed for power training.

T 27. The pyramid system was so named since the technique was developed in Egypt by their Olympic team.

T 28. Females can produce the same force per unit cross–sectional area of muscle as males.

T 29. A leg extension is the same as a concentric contraction of the quadriceps muscles.

F 30. Since fat can only be burned aerobically, you cannot lose body fat by lifting weights.

66 F 31. Flexibility has three components: neural, mechanical, and tangential.

F 32. If you are 20 pounds overweight you must have a high percentage of body fat.

82-83 F 33. A person's basal metabolic rate (BMR) can best be defined as the amount of energy it will take he or she to do one single rep of an exercise.

F 34. Vitamins are a good source of calories.

Part 2: Matching

A 35. Bench press   A Pectoralis major, triceps
I 36. Supine overhead dumbbell raise   B Lower back (erector spinae)
F 37. Leg extension   C Obliques
E 38. Leg curl   D Biceps brachii
G 39. Shoulder shrug   E Hamstrings
H 40. Lateral raise   F Quadriceps
D 41. Preacher curl   G Upper trapezius
K 42. French press   H Deltoids
C 43. Cross crunch   I Latissimus dorsi
B 44. Stiff leg dead lift   J Gastrocnemius and soleus
J 45. Toe raise   K Triceps brachii

Part 3: Multiple Choice

46. The structure which directly reacts to prevent a ballistic stretch is:
    a) Long bone
    b) Golgi tendon organ
    c) Muscle spindle
    d) Myosin molecule

47. You should start your workout by drinking approximately 16 ounces of water and supplement this with four to six ounces:
    a) Every hour
    b) Every 15 minutes
    c) Every two hours
    d) Every day

48. All of the following are results of steroid use except:
    a) Larger muscle mass
    b) More high density lipoproteins
    c) Liver damage
    d) Increased blood pressure

49. All of the following exercises will use the deltoids except:
    a) Lateral raises
    b) Overhead press
    c) Inclined press
    d) Seated rows

50. All of the following exercises will use the biceps brachii except:
    a) Lateral raises
    b) Lat pulldowns
    c) Preacher curls
    d) Seated rows

51. All of the following exercises are extensions except:
    a) Leg curls
    b) Leg press
    c) Overhead press
    d) Bench press

52. Which of the following goals cannot be accomplished through weight training:
    a) Improved sports performance
    b) Aerobic improvements
    c) Conversion of fat to muscle
    d) Increased power

53. Fast twitch muscle must have all of the following properties except:
    a) Fast contractile speed
    b) A large amount of actin and myosin
    c) Large volume of glycolytic enzymes
    d) A large volume of mitochondria

54. A "negative" set is a series of the following type of contractions:
    a) Eccentric
    b) Isometric
    c) Isokinetic
    d) Introspective

55. The prime mover in an adduction of the arm is:
    a) Biceps brachii
    b) Deltoid
    c) Triceps brachii
    d) Gastrocnemius

56. Since the human body is composed of bony levers which have longer resistance arms than force arms, it is designed for:
    a) Strength
    b) Energy
    c) Range of motion
    d) Static force production

57. The following machine uses cams or levers to change resistance according to the angle of pull of the muscle being exercised:
   a) Accommodating resistance
   b) Isokinetic
   c) Isolateral
   d) Extensive resistance

58. All of the following statements are advantages of machines over free weights except:
   a) Strengthening of accessory muscles
   b) No need for spotters
   c) Weight control through range of motion
   d) Excellent isolation for specific muscles

59. All of the following exercises have the same prime mover except:
   a) Flies
   b) Lat pull downs
   c) Flat bench press
   d) Inclined bench press

60. All of the following exercises work the quadriceps group except:
   a) Squat
   b) Leg extension
   c) Toe raise
   d) Leg press

61. The targeted muscle in the chin–up is:
   a) Triceps brachii
   b) Pectoralis major
   c) Deltoid
   d) Latissimus dorsi

62. The thing not to do when stretching is:
   a) Warm up the muscle
   b) Stretch slowly
   c) Bounce into the stretch
   d) Hold a stretch 15 seconds

63. The cat stretches concentrate on the:
   a) Lower back
   b) Quadriceps
   c) Shoulder girdle
   d) Gastrocnemius and soleus

64. Which of the following weight training techniques would you recommend to a competitive shotputter?
   a) Super sets
   b) Power cleans
   c) Super circuit
   d) Progressive fatigue system

65. Energy can best be defined as the:
   a) Amount of fuel available for workouts
   b) Maximum weight you can move
   c) Maximum speed you can move
   d) Maximum resistance during an exercise

Part 4: Fill in the Blanks

A contraction involving no movement is called (66.)_____.

A machine that adjusts the resistance to allow for differences in strength at different joint angles is called (67.)_____.

The bench used to isolate the biceps brachii is called the
(68.) _Preacher_ bench.
The best known accommodating resistance machine is the
(69) _Nautilus_.
The speed at which you can perform a lift can be defined as
(70) _Power_.
The five variables that you can manipulate in a weight training program
are:
(71.) _intensity_   (74.) _speed_
(72.) _frequency_   (75.) _specific exercise (specificity)_
(73.) _duration_
(76.) The theory that a muscle will change exactly as the exercise
dictates it should is called _specificity of adaptation (training)_
One complete movement of an exercise is called a (77.) _rep_.
A specific number of these movements is called (78.) _set_.
The two ways a muscle can increase in size are (79.) _hypertrophy_ and
(80.) _hyperplasia_.
The two lifts commonly performed by Olympic lifters are
(81.) _two-hand snatch_ and (82.) _two-hand clean & jerk_
When training swimmers, a commonly used advanced training technique is
(83.) _high speed concentric only system_
Carbohydrate should make up between (84.) _60_ and
(85.) _75_ percent of your daily dietary intake.
The loss of bone with advancing age is called (86.) _osteoporosis_.
The two major multi–joint exercises performed by power athletes are
(87.) _Snatch_ and (88.) _power clean_
The first lifter to perform progressive resistance was reported to be
(89.) _Milo of Crotona_; however, a progressive resistance exercise
system was first prescribed by (90.) _T.L. Delorme_.
Human skeletal muscle is approximately (91.) _25%_ percent
efficient while human cardiac muscle has an efficiency rating of about
(92.) _50%_ percent.
Among the most common problems experienced by athletes using steroids
are:
(93.) _increased blood pressure_   (94.) _decreased HDL, increased LDL_
(95.) _liver damage_   (96.) _decreased female sex hormone_
The structures in the muscle that tell it to make new protein and increase in
size are (97.) _nuclei_. The structures that make new muscle
fibers are (98.) _satellite cells_
When we examine weight training as a form of exercise to be done by
specific groups of people, we can truly say that weight training is for
(99.) _everyone_.

INDEX